THE VERBAL REASONING TEST WORKBOOK

Unbeatable practice for verbal ability, English, usage and interpretation and judgement tests

MIKE BRYON

KOGAN PAGE

London and Philadelphia

Whilst the author has made every effort to ensure that the content of this book is accurate, please note that occasional errors can occur in books of this kind. If you suspect that an error has been made in any of the tests included in this book, please inform the publishers at the address printed below so that it can be corrected at the next reprint.

Publisher's note
Every possible effort has been made to ensure that the information contained in this book is accurate at the time of going to press, and the publishers and author cannot accept responsibility for any errors or omissions, however caused. No responsibility for loss or damage occasioned to any person acting, or refraining from action, as a result of the material in this publication can be accepted by the editor, the publisher or the author.

First published in Great Britain and the United States in 2008 by Kogan Page Limited.

120 Pentonville Road
London N1 9JN
United Kingdom
www.koganpage.com

525 South 4th Street, #241
Philadelphia PA 19147
USA

© Mike Bryon, 2008

The right of Mike Bryon to be identified as the author of this work has been asserted by him in accordance with the Copyright, Designs and Patents Act 1988.

ISBN 978 0 7494 5150 9

British Library Cataloguing-in-Publication Data
A CIP record for this book is available from the British Library.

Library of Congress Cataloging-in-Publication Data
Bryon, Mike.
    The verbal reasoning test workbook : unbeatable practice for verbal ability, English usage and interpretation and judgement tests / Mike Bryon.
        p. cm.
    ISBN 978-0-7494-5150-9
    1. Verbal ability--Examinations, questions, etc. 2. Reasoning (Psychology) --
Examinations, questions, etc. 3. Employment tests--Examinations, questions, etc. I. Title.
    BF463.V45B795 2008
    153.9'3--dc22
                                    2008007987

Typeset by Saxon Graphics Ltd, Derby
Printed and bound in Great Britain by MPG Books Ltd, Bodmin, Cornwall

THE VERBAL REASONING TEST WORKBOOK

Contents

Contents

Preface

Everything you need for a successful programme of self-study

If you face a test of your verbal reasoning but lack practice or confidence and have been searching for help then you have found it. This book provides all you need to undertake a major programme of self-study and get some valuable test practice without the pressure of a job offer hanging on your performance. All you have to do is settle down somewhere quiet and get practising. Very soon you will be more confident, much faster at answering these questions and achieve a much higher score. Now is the time to get down to some serious study and overcome your anxieties. To succeed you may need to work harder than some of your colleagues but if you really go for it then you will triumph.

First make sure you adopt the winning mindset detailed in Chapter 1, and at the earliest opportunity find out about the type of questions that make up the test you face. Next, work through Chapters 2 and 3. Allow yourself sufficient time to practise, especially on the bits of the test that represent the greatest challenge to you. Now get down to lots more score-improving practice on the realistic practice questions provided in Chapters 4 and 5. Finally, practise under realistic test conditions in

Chapter 6. As you go along check your answers, review the explanations and interpret your scores in Chapter 7.

I have signposted sources of further practice available in the Kogan Page Testing Series so that you can continue your programme of revision and be prepared for all types of tests and all levels of difficulty.

Each chapter starts with easier material and gets progressively harder. You will find therefore that the questions in an actual test are more difficult than the questions at the beginning of each chapter. This is intentional as it helps ensure that you build up to the level required to do well in a verbal reasoning test at the intermediate level.

You can find out more about the further suggested reading at mikebryon.com. If you face a test that contains questions of a type not covered by this book, then by all means contact me via help@mikebryon.com and I will be glad to let you know of a source of suitable practice material.

May I take this opportunity to wish you every success in passing your next psychometric test of verbal reasoning.

1

Adopt the winning approach

This book is intended for the reader who faces a test of verbal reasoning at the intermediate level and who lacks either practice or confidence in the fundamental skills. If the grammar classes of school are a distant or bad memory, if tests of verbal reasoning are your worst nightmare, then this is the book for you. You will not find another title with so many verbal reasoning practice questions. If you are preparing for advanced verbal reasoning tests, make sure you move onto the hundreds of questions found in the Kogan Page title, *How To Pass Advanced Verbal Reasoning Tests* once you have completed this workbook.

We face tests at so many points in our life: at school, increasingly when we apply for jobs or courses and at work when we apply for promotion or a career move. Employers and course administrators are looking for all-round candidates and those with a balanced set of essential skills including verbal reasoning skills. Tests are used to distinguish between the candidates with or without these skills. You will come across a verbal reasoning paper in most psychometric tests that are used today.

You may be weak verbally but great in other skill areas, for example you might have very strong numeracy skills. You will no doubt be given the opportunity to demonstrate these in another part of the assessment, but to guarantee success you have to pass all the sub-tests that make up a psychometric assessment. If you neglect the verbal test hoping to rely on a high score in your area of personal strength then you run the risk of being rejected.

Everyone can pass

The good news is that you will pass these tests if you make the necessary commitment. It takes some people longer to reach that point. Some candidates have to work much harder, but that applies to most things in life. We all have our personal strengths and weaknesses. You have found this book so all you now need to succeed is time, determination and some hard work. To master these skills and to make the necessary commitment can be really boring, painful even, but if success is important then you have no real alternative but to get on with it.

Put aside any feeling of resentment

Perhaps you know that you can do the job, and naturally ask yourself why you have to pass a test. You might wonder what relevance it has to the role to which you have applied. These are understandable and common sentiments. But you really must try to put them aside as they are counterproductive and will serve only to distract you from the real task at hand, namely passing the test. To do this you have to adopt the right mental approach. If you turn up on the day harbouring resentments then you are unlikely to demonstrate your true potential. The winning candidate concentrates not on the threat or inconvenience but instead on the opportunity the test represents. Pass it and you can go on to realize your personal goals.

See the test as a chance to show how strong a candidate you really are. Attend fully prepared, confident in your own ability and ready to succeed. Understand that doing well in a test is not simply a matter of intelligence but also requires determination and hard work. If passing is important to you then be prepared to set aside a significant number of hours in which to practise, and to work very hard during the real test.

If you have faced failure in the past, if you have previously tried and failed to master these skills, then it will take courage to make the necessary commitment.

The importance of practice

You must seek to achieve the best possible score in the test. Other candidates will be trying to do this, so you must too. The secret is practice and for many candidates it will mean the difference between pass and fail. Practice works best on material that is as much like the questions in the real test as possible – treat them as if they were the real thing. Where necessary obtain further material from other titles in the Kogan Page Testing Series.

Practise right up to the day before the test. To ensure that you are continuing to improve, the practice must remain a challenge. If it stops being a pain then there really will be very little gain! However, before you start practising you must get 'test wise'.

Get test wise

As soon as you are told that you need to pass a test of verbal reasoning try to find out as much as you can. The organization that has invited you should provide you with, or direct you to, a description of the test and some sample questions. You will not be able to get hold of past papers or real copies of the test.

Most tests comprise a series of shorter tests taken one after the other with a short pause between the papers. They might include a sub-test on verbal reasoning, then a numerical reasoning sub-test and finally a non-verbal reasoning sub-test. But this is only one of many possible combinations. The series of sub-tests are called a 'battery'. It is really important that you understand exactly what each part of the test involves. You will be astonished at how many people attend a test without knowing what to expect. The first time they learn about the type of questions is when the test administrator describes them just before the test begins for real. Don't make this mistake. You need to know the nature of the challenge as soon as possible. Get details on:

- how many sub-tests the test battery comprises;
- what the title of each sub-test is;
- what sort of question makes up a sub-test (find an example of each type of question);
- how many questions each sub-test includes;
- how long you are allowed to complete each sub-test;
- whether it is multiple-choice or short answer;
- whether you complete it with pen and paper or at a computer terminal;
- whether there is a numeracy paper and if a calculator is allowed.

Once you have a clear idea of the test you face you need to set about finding hundreds of relevant practice questions. If you struggle in verbal tests then you will have to practise a lot. This book contains 700 questions. In the Kogan Page series you will find complementary publications that offer lots more practice and alternative explanations of the key competencies. There are also titles containing advanced material on verbal and numerical tests and specialist titles intended for particular tests such as those for the Police, Fire Service or UK Civil Service.

To obtain more practice material for verbal tests at the intermediate level I recommend *The Ultimate Psychometric Test Book* and *How to Pass Selection Tests*. For practice for numerical tests at the intermediate level use *The Numeracy Test Workbook*. At the graduate and advanced level verbal tests I propose *How to Pass Graduate Psychometric Tests, The Graduate Psychometric Test Workbook* and *How to Pass Advanced Verbal Reasoning Tests*. For numerical tests at the advanced level I suggest *How to Pass Advanced Numeracy Tests* and *The Advanced Numeracy Test Workbook*. All these titles are published by Kogan Page and you will find descriptions of them at www.mikebryon.com.

Special situations

If you suffer a disability

If you suffer a disability that will adversely affect your ability to complete a test or any aspect of a recruitment process then inform the organization concerned at the first opportunity. It should be prepared to organize things differently to better accommodate your needs, and for certain conditions may allow extra time to complete the test.

If you suffer from dyslexia then a test of verbal reasoning can represent a significant obstacle. Inform the organization that has invited you for the test of your condition. Many organizations will allow dyslexic candidates extra time to complete the test but they are likely to want proof that you are indeed dyslexic. If you have not already obtained a formal assessment then now is the time to get one. This will involve meeting an educational psychologist or other trained professional who will assess you and provide a written report of his or her findings. This process can take some weeks and it is for this reason that I suggest that you inform the organization straight away. The cost of such an assessment can be a quite significant sum and that cost is very likely to be yours. If you are dyslexic then with practice you can still greatly improve your performance in these common tests and pass.

After the test the organization should be willing to provide information on your performance, although you may have to ask for it. It should indicate the areas in which you performed most strongly and areas in which you might work to improve. Some will be willing to discuss your score with you over the telephone; this is often the way to get the most valuable feedback.

If English is not your first language

Tests of verbal reasoning are likely to present a great challenge to you if your first language is not English, and you need to adjust your programme of revision accordingly. For a speaker of English as a second language the reading comprehension and critical reading style of question (see Chapter 5) are likely to prove the most challenging. You might actually find yourself at an advantage in tests of English usage (see Chapter 4) as many native speakers of English have forgotten or never formally learnt the rules of English grammar.

To meet the challenge of a verbal reasoning test and in particular the reading comprehension and critical reading style of question, at an early stage – if possible daily – spend time reading quality newspapers and journals. This will help build your vocabulary and improve your proficiency at assimilating the meanings of the complex sentences and sentence structures that occur in these tests. Look up unfamiliar words. Practise writing 70-word reviews of articles found in these publications.

Be prepared to undertake a sizeable amount of practice prior to the real test. Practice will help you achieve a considerably better score so start early and make a significant commitment in terms of the time spent practising on realistic material. For many non-native speakers of English, practice will mean the difference between success and disappointment.

Remember to be really disciplined at looking up the meaning of words with which you are unfamiliar.

If you left school or college many years ago

If it is quite some time since you studied, and in particular since you studied English grammar, then a verbal reasoning test may well present a number of specific hurdles.

The first thing to do is to review examples of each type of question you face in the real test and make an honest assessment of which of these components represent the greatest challenge for you. Well before sitting the test you will need to begin a programme of revision. Start with the aspects of the test that you feel you are least good at. If your test is online or taken on a computer at a centre you only need minimal knowledge of IT, but make sure that you are confident about your keyboard skills.

You can practise taking a computer-administered test using the Kogan Page CD-ROM, *How to Pass Psychometric Tests Volume 1*. Ideally, revise over a number of months, aiming at 10 hours a week of practice. Without undertaking such a programme you could risk not achieving a good score. Making the necessary commitment will demand a high degree of motivation. The time spent practising will occasionally seem tedious and frustrating. For many people revising grammar or verbal reasoning is not what they dream of doing in their spare time, but push ahead with it because it really will make a difference to your score in an actual test.

Work to redevelop a good exam technique. This demands a balance between speed and accuracy. Some very good candidates will need to unlearn a thoughtful, considered approach. You can actually think too deeply or take too few risks in a verbal test. Practise under the pressure of time at realistic questions; where appropriate look at the suggested answers for clues; and practise informed guessing (where you can eliminate some of the suggested answers and then guess from those that remain).

On a positive note, practice should afford you a marked improvement in your performance. Your work history may also have prepared you well for any reading comprehension and critical reading style of questions.

What to expect on the day

You may well be invited to attend a training or recruitment centre to take the test, but it could just as likely be online at a computer away from a centre. If taken at a centre the test may either be administered with paper and pen or at a computer screen. However the test is administered, it will be a multiple-choice or short answer test. You will either be presented with a selection of suggested answers from which you are expected to select the correct one, or you will be asked to record your answer in the space provided.

If the test is at a centre, don't be late! And dress smartly. You are likely to be one of many candidates attending that day. You may be expected to attend for some hours and it is possible that you will be required to complete a whole series of exercises. All this detail will be included in your letter of invitation, so read it carefully.

Remember that doing well in any test requires hard work and determination. If at the end of the day you do not feel completely exhausted then you may not have done yourself justice. So go for it.

Make sure you are in the right frame of mind on the day. Remember the winning approach and look forward to the challenge and the opportunity it represents. You are there to demonstrate your abilities and prove to the organization that you are a suitable candidate. Attend the test fully prepared having spent many hours practising and having addressed any areas of weakness. Do not underestimate how long it can take to prepare for a test. Start as soon as you receive notice that you must attend.

Obviously you must listen carefully to the instructions provided before a test begins, but appreciate that you may well be feeling nervous, which may affect your concentration, so make yourself focus on what is being said. Much of the information will be a repeat of the test description sent to you with the invitation to sit the test, so read and reread this document before the day of the test.

Pay particular attention to instructions on how many questions there are in each sub-test and be sure you are familiar with the demands of each style of question. Does it say 'turn over' at the bottom of the page? You will be surprised how many people reach the bottom of a page and wrongly conclude that they have reached the end of the questions. They stop working and wait when they should be working away at the remaining questions.

Keep track of the time during the test and manage how long you spend on any one question. You must keep going right up to the end. Aim to get the balance right between speed and accuracy. It is better that you risk getting some questions wrong but attempt every question, rather than double-checking each answer and being told to stop because you have run out of time before you have finished. Practice can really help develop this skill.

If you hit a difficult section of questions don't lose heart. Keep going – everyone gets some questions wrong. You may find that you come to another section of questions at which you can excel.

If you do not know the answer to a question then educated guessing is well worth a try. If you are unsure of an answer to a multiple-choice question, look at the suggested answers and try ruling some out that seem wrong. In this way you will reduce the number of suggested answers from which to choose and hopefully increase your chances of guessing correctly.

2

150 warm-up questions

The questions in this chapter are organized as three practice types that develop your verbal reasoning, vocabulary, comprehension and knowledge of English usage. Mixed in amongst the three types are also direct questions of usage – questions that ask you to identify, for example, the subject or the adjective in a sentence.

You may not face these styles of question in a real test of verbal reasoning but they will help you develop the competencies, knowledge, confidence and speed necessary to do well in this type of test. These warm-up questions will help prepare you for the real thing.

In verbal reasoning tests language is used in a far more precise way than in everyday speech. The questions that make up the test rely on fine distinctions between meaning and only one of the suggested answers is deemed correct. You must adopt the same precise approach or risk being judged wrong. The sort of practice in this chapter will help you develop the necessary precision and go on to get a far better score.

You should expect to get the vast majority of these questions right. If you find that you cannot attain this level of accuracy then be prepared to undertake a quite significant amount of practice to ensure that you realize the standard demanded by employers in their verbal reasoning tests.

You should work quickly and aim to reach the point where you can answer each question in 30 seconds.

Find the new word

Your task is to find a four or five letter word or words that are made up by combining the last few letters of one of the given words with the first few letters of the next word. Most of the answers are everyday terms with which you are entirely familiar. No archaic or informal words, abbreviations or regional spellings are used.

1. Eskimo   vertical   painkiller   **Answer** [   ]

2. diamond   espresso   message   **Answer** [   ]

    di   dome

3. Identify the abstract noun in the following sentence:

    At camp Peter found the idea of the cold water shower just as bad as the experience.

    Idea   Water   Camp   Peter

                                        Answer [   ]

4. fence   Christmas   talent   *m*   **Answer** [*earl*]
          hease ce   was   letal eta
                                    ustal
                                    east

5. Eurostar   tennis   justice   **Answer** [*mas*]

6. Which word in the following sentence is a conditional expression?

    We have been invited to a party and really should go.

                                        Answer [*really*]

7. assistant   humble   asylum   **Answer** [*table*]
          ta   tuhle

8. exorcize   round   giveaway   **Answer** [   ]

          zero

9. minimum   evening   lasso   **Answer** [ ]

    Minimum evenslo

10. Identify the word that serves as a conjunction in the sentence:

    I was enjoying a relaxing bath when the phone rang.

    Answer [ ]

11. evaporate   lloyd   philosophy   **Answer** [ ]

12. dictionary   frost   archery   **Answer** [ ]

    dictionary frost archery

13. Identify the comparative word or phrase in the sentence:

    I am older than my sister.

    Answer [ ]

14. curfew   illegal   reject   **Answer** [ ]

    curfew illegal reject

15. outpost   irritant   spangle   **Answer** [Stir]

    Out post irritant Spangle

16. Identify the adverb in the sentence:

    He gently fitted the picture into the frame.

    Answer [ ]

    Stir

17. heavy   flamingo   attack   **Answer**

18. feather   evolve   technical   **Answer**

19. Which of the following contractions means you have?

    You're   You've   You'll   You'd

    Answer

20. electric   horrid   cluster   **Answer**

21. Identify the collective noun in the following sentence:

    The swarm of bees chased after the two unfortunate dogs.

    Answer

22. gumbo   thorn   idiot   **Answer**

23. okra   sparrow   dissolve   **Answer**

24. forensic   knowledge   terrace   **Answer**

25. Identify the active verb in the following sentence:

    The erupting volcano had last erupted over 400 years ago.

    Erupting   Volcano   Erupted   Years   Ago

    Answer [   ]

26. though   erode   pistol   **Answer** [   ]

27. cucumber   fatwa   itinerary   **Answer** [   ]

    cucumberfatwaitinerary

28. froth   animal   tourist   **Answer** [   ]

29. dangling   amendment   darkroom   **Answer** [   ]

30. How many concrete nouns does the following sentence contain?

    He added milk and sugar to his coffee but it still tasted bitter.

    Answer [   ]

31. classic   divided   awning   **Answer** [*dawn*]

    classicdividedawning

32. specific   ultrasound   injection   **Answer** [*Culture*]

    specificultrasoundinjection

33. Which of the following nouns are countable?

Mammal   Tree   Bird   Mushroom   Shark

Answer [   ]

34. philology   rotund   injury   **Answer** [   ]

35. scheme   experimental   eruption   **Answer** [   ]

36. How many adjectives does the following sentence include?

She found the psychometric test almost impossible.

Answer [   ]

37. resist   diesel   fizzle   **Answer** [   ]

38. harmonica   method   subsist   **Answer** [   ]

39. Canada   shackle   wastage   **Answer** [   ]

40. Which of the following articles are demonstrative?

This   The   That   Or   Can

Answer [   ]

41. skit   entitle   brilliant   **Answer** [   ]

42. barrage   sandbar   kitchen   **Answer** [   ]

43. How many conditional expressions does the following sentence contain?

    I would exercise more often if I had more time.

    Answer [   ]

44. flush   otherwise   count   **Answer** [   ]

45. jelly   toast   oilfield   **Answer** [   ]

46. metabolism   essence   array   **Answer** [   ]

47. carbon   estate   stigma   **Answer** [   ]

48. dentist   ewe   loose   **Answer** [Stew]
    dentisteweloose

49. general   idea   fear   **Answer** [   ]
    Stewel

50. weight   dead   emotional   **Answer** [demo]
    weight deademotional

Word link – opposites

In the case of this style of question your task is to find the word in the list that is the opposite of the word at the top. Doing well in these questions is all about possessing a wide vocabulary and having the confidence to use it. If you find them very easy that is fantastic, but don't make the mistake of not practising. Use these questions to develop a winning exam technique. In most tests there are far more questions than the time allows you to answer. The high scoring candidate will be the one who can get the right answer without double-checking or taking much time to reflect on the suggested answers. So do not make the mistake of thinking you will achieve a high score in the real test because you can do well in these questions without the pressure of time.

Be sure to look up in a dictionary any words you do not know.

51. shallow

    A   serious
    B   frivolous
    C   grave   **Answer**

52. Identify the active verb in the following sentence:

    After I was told that the old road was closed I spent the afternoon telling people the news.

    A   After
    B   Was told
    C   Telling
    D   News   **Answer**

53. understanding

    A   familiarity
    B   ignorance
    C   expertise   **Answer**

54. departure

    A   capture
    B   admit
    C   entrance   **Answer**

55. divide

    A   separate
    B   unify
    C   share-out   **Answer**

56. covert

  A   open
  B   reveal
  C   close   **Answer**

57. How many concrete nouns does the sentence contain?

  He loved the mountains and day-dreamed of climbing snow covered peaks.

  Answer   3

58. intricate

  A   general
  B   inexact
  C   large   **Answer**

59. Identify the suggested answer that makes a comparative word or phrase in the sentence:

  I found the book more enjoyable than the film.

  1   More
  2   Enjoyable
  3   More enjoyable
  4   Than the film   **Answer**   3

60. count

  A   recite
  B   total
  C   commoner   **Answer**

61. Identify the adverb in the following sentence:

    I will book the flights tomorrow.

    Answer

62. square

    (A) dishonest
    B multiply
    C dance   **Answer**

63. steep

    A oversupply
    B reasonable
    C saturate   **Answer**

64. Which of the following is written in the imperative?

    1 I will have finished by this afternoon.
    2 What would you buy if you won the lottery?
    3 Another bus will be arriving any moment now.
    4 Bring me a newspaper.

                                          Answer 4

65. blunt

    A uncompromised
    B point
    C weaken   **Answer** B

66. loathe

    A deplore
    B abhor
    C adore

    Answer   C

67. What is the meaning of the contraction 'we're'?

    1 We had
    2 We would
    3 We have
    4 We will
    5 We are

    Answer   5

68. ruin

    A undo
    B raise
    C mar

    Answer   B

69. ascendant

    A assertive
    B dominant
    C subservient

    Answer   C

70. fast

    A eat
    B speedy
    C tight

    Answer   4

71. resistant

  A   susceptible
  B   immune
  C   sensitive

  Answer A

72. exclude

  A   invoke
  B   involve
  C   invite

  Answer B

73. animate

  A   vigorate
  (B) depress
  C   mock

  Answer B

74. commute

  A   home worker
  B   travel
  C   increase

  Answer C

75. Identify the collective noun in the following sentence:

  The team of football players were late for the match.

  Answer team

76. concession

  A   denial
  B   allowance
  C   surrender

  Answer B

77. defect

    A   desert

    B   spotless

    C   traitor   **Answer**   B

78. Which of the following nouns are countable?

    Space

    Water

    People

    Idea   **Answer**   Idea

79. peripheral

    A   central

    B   secondary

    C   incidental   **Answer**   A

80. intractable

    tract

    A   stubborn

    B   difficult

    C   compliant   **Answer**   A

81. tail

    A   shadow

    B   fade

    C   start   **Answer**   C

82. soil

    A   foul

    B   medium

    C   spotless   **Answer**

83. Identify the abstract noun in the following sentence:

The height of the mountain as well as its sheer rock face made it a very difficult climb.

                                         Answer

84. tender

    A   sympathetic

    B   annoy

    C   withdraw   **Answer**

85. wasteful

    A   profligate

    B   thrifty

    C   profuse   **Answer**

86. elongate

    A   horizontal

    B   abridge

    C   prolong   **Answer**

87. Indicate which of the suggested answers serves as a comparative word or phrase in the sentence:

    She was the smaller of the two but she was the bravest.

    1   Smaller
    2   The two
    3   The bravest   **Answer**

88. orthodox

    A   disposition
    B   religion
    C   wrong   **Answer**

89. Identify the conjunction in the following sentence:

    I still enjoyed myself despite the fact that I ate too much and felt rather unwell.

                             Answer

90. prone

    A   upright
    B   lying flat
    C   tendency   **Answer**

91. neglect

    A   disposed
    B   tend
    C   compassionate   **Answer**

92. unlimited

    A   liability

    B   heterogeneous

    C   finite   **Answer**

93. ceaselessly

    A   seldom

    B   always

    C   ample   **Answer**

94. How many adjectives does the following sentence contain?

The children were cheeky but cheerful.

                                      Answer

95. contemporary

    A   anarchic

    B   outmoded

    C   ancestor   **Answer**

96. slump

    A   boom

    B   decline

    C   explosion   **Answer**

97. lend

    A   lone

    B   single

    C   borrow   **Answer**

98. possibly

    A   certainty
    B   negative
    C   positive   **Answer**

99. resemble

    A   agree
    B   differ
    C   contrast   **Answer**

100. miserable

    A   euphoric
    B   effusive
    C   eclectic   **Answer**

Word link – synonyms

In this style of question your task is to find two words that are closest in meaning or with the strongest connection. As with the last style of question this sort are also a test of your vocabulary and your confidence in it. Reading widely and practice are the key to doing well in tests of this sort. If you get any of the following questions wrong then be sure to look up the word in a dictionary. Try the following 50 examples.

101. isolate

    A   alienate
    B   switch
    C   annex   **Answer**

102. lineage

    A   accord
    B   attach
    C   ancestry   **Answer**

103. Which of the following are examples of the superlative form?

    Youngest
    Slowest
    Most liked
    Happiest   **Answer**

104. abundant

    A   prolong
    B   propagate
    C   prolific   **Answer**

105. utter

    A   greatest
    B   vocalize
    C   nonsense   **Answer**

106. Identify the adverb in the following sentence:

     They had visited the city once before.

     Answer [   ]

107. common

     A   banal
     B   canal
     C   baleful   **Answer** [   ]

108. Which of the following contractions means will not?

     1   Wasn't
     2   Weren't
     3   Won't
     4   Wouldn't   **Answer** [   ]

109. caricature

     A   criticism
     B   cartoon
     C   concoction   **Answer** [   ]

110. debilitate

     A   weaken
     B   corrupt
     C   deflate   **Answer** [   ]

111. If there is one, identify the conditional expression in the following sentence:

What do you plan to do if the weather is bad?

Answer [ ]

112. elicit

    A   stop
    B   allow
    C   obtain

Answer [ ]

113. Identify the collective noun in the following sentence:

My eldest brother could not come but otherwise my whole family attended the ceremony.

Answer [ ]

114. facility

    A   division
    B   amenity
    C   disposition   **Answer** [ ]

115. general

    A   comprehensive
    B   undisputed
    C   straightforward   **Answer** [ ]

116. occur

    A   confront

    B   concur

    C   ensue   **Answer**

117. insight

    A   perception

    B   adamant

    C   look over   **Answer**

118. How many concrete nouns does the following sentence contain?

    The car park has space for 25 vehicles.

                                   Answer

119. type

    A   actual

    B   genuine

    C   class   **Answer**

120. Which if any of the following is the contraction meaning am not?

    Aren't

    Am'n

    Amn't

    None of these   **Answer**

121. usually

    A   completely
    B   ordinarily
    C   actually   **Answer**

122. alike

    A   same
    B   twin
    C   identical   **Answer**

123. Which word in the sentence is the conjunction?

    I called at the post office because I needed to buy some stamps.

                                Answer

124. important

    A   principle
    B   predominance
    C   principal   **Answer**

125. gone

    A   over
    B   more
    C   here   **Answer**

126. earliest

    A   best
    B   first
    C   prime   **Answer**

127. A synonym of the word 'mean' when used as a verb is:

   A   signify
   B   midpoint
   C   miserly   **Answer**

128. advantageous

   A   reasonable
   B   fair
   C   favourable   **Answer**

129. eye

   A   sense
   B   observe
   C   appraise   **Answer**

130. uncertainty

   A   doubt
   B   disbelieve
   C   suspicion   **Answer**

131. approach

   A   surface
   B   progress
   C   come   **Answer**

132. low-cost

   A   cheep
   B   economical
   C   ashamed   **Answer**

133. be

    A   happening

    B   through

    C   exist   **Answer**

134. Identify the abstract noun in the following sentence:

The children found mathematics difficult and their maths teacher Mr Right unsympathetic.

                                    Answer

135. since

    A   as

    B   if

    C   to   **Answer**

136. How many adjectives does the following sentence contain?

The blue car was very technical and far more advanced than the yellow one it was parked next to.

                                      Answer

137. fallacious

    A   invention

    B   illusion

    C   mistaken   **Answer**

138. double

    A   duplicity
    B   dual
    C   betrayal   **Answer**

139. ply

    A   use
    B   shell
    C   sell   **Answer**

140. The noun refuse means:

    A   withhold
    B   rubbish
    C   decline   **Answer**

141. definite

    A   specific
    B   universal
    C   vague   **Answer**

142. faint

    A   sick
    B   unstipulated
    C   indistinct   **Answer**

143. sequence

    A   rope
    B   string
    C   warp   **Answer**

144. Identify the active verb in the following sentence:

The guy in the swimming pool was in trouble and calling out but no one helped.

Swimming
Trouble
Calling
Helped   **Answer**

145. opt

    A   consider
    B   choose
    C   ponder   **Answer**

146. arduous

    A   distinguish
    B   divergent
    C   difficult   **Answer**

147. guarantee

    A   ensue
    B   ensure
    C   entail   **Answer**

148. establish

    A   prove
    B   accept
    C   attempt   **Answer**

149. As an adjective, intimate means:

    A   proclaim
    B   divulge
    C   close   **Answer**

150. Which of the follow nouns is countable?

    Dog
    Art
    Cloth
    Sea weed   **Answer**

3

150 verbal reasoning questions

This chapter contains practice in three styles of verbal reasoning question. Tests comprising these styles of question are less common than they used to be but they are still prevalent. If you are applying for a range of jobs then at some stage you are bound to face a test based on these sorts of questions. Practice will make a big difference to your performance.

Even if you do not face a test of this type, use this material to develop a good exam technique, to develop your vocabulary and the necessary careful, precise approach to meaning essential for a top score in these tests. If you prefer to take these exercises against the clock, allow yourself 30 seconds per question.

Synonyms and antonyms mixed up – this makes the questions harder

In the warm-up chapter you undertook almost 100 questions of this sort but in this chapter synonym and antonym questions are mixed up. In a real test of this type you will face both synonym and antonym questions in the same test. The question setter will try to deliberately mislead you by offering both as suggested answers – they do this in the expectation that you will forget the task and identify, say, the synonym rather than the antonym as the answer.

Even if you do not face a test of this kind, don't skip this section because this sort of practice really helps develop the precise use of language that verbal reasoning tests demand.

Use the following 50 examples to become completely familiar with this sort of question.

1. Which of the following is a synonym of dry?

    A   wet
    B   dull
    C   blunt   **Answer**

2. Which of the following is a synonym of part?

    A   involvement
    B   association
    C   interest   **Answer**

3. Find the antonym of fast.

    A   loose
    B   rapid
    C   promiscuous   **Answer**

4. Which of the following is a synonym of few?

    A   plenty
    B   not many
    C   less   **Answer**

5. Find the antonym of loss.

    A   saved
    B   vanish
    C   profit   **Answer**

6. Find the antonym of dawn.

    A   evening
    B   day break
    C   end   **Answer**

7. Which of the following is a synonym of continue?

   A impede
   B last
   C final   **Answer** [   ]

8. Which of the following is a synonym of go?

   A given
   B fetch
   C arrive   **Answer** [   ]

9. Find the antonym of ponder.

   A discount
   B money off
   C concession   **Answer** [   ]

10. Which of the following is an antonym of instant?

   A express
   B delayed
   C occasion   **Answer** [   ]

11. Which of the following is a synonym of pull?

   A repel
   B record
   C remove   **Answer** [   ]

12. Which of the following is a synonym of take?

   A subtract
   B free
   C pack   **Answer** [   ]

13. Which of the following is an antonym of stale?

    A   outdated

    B   impasse

    C   original   **Answer**

14. Which of the following is a synonym of very?

    A   numerous

    B   extremely

    C   slightly   **Answer**

15. Find the antonym of intransigent.

    A   pliable

    B   stubborn

    C   wilful   **Answer**

16. Which of the following is a synonym of deal?

    A   survive

    B   bring

    C   cope   **Answer**

17. Find the antonym of idealistic.

    A   naive

    B   realistic

    C   optimistic   **Answer**

18. Find the antonym of exhibit.

    A   concede

    B   cancel

    C   conceal   **Answer**

19. Which of the following is a synonym of close?

    A   clinch
    B   begin
    C   down   **Answer**

20. Which of the following is a synonym of put?

    A   fast
    B   express
    C   swift   **Answer**

21. Which of the following is an antonym of broad?

    A   detailed
    B   expansive
    C   expensive   **Answer**

22. Which of the following is a synonym of set?

    A   askew
    B   uncertain
    C   adjust   **Answer**

23. Which of the following is an antonym of emit?

    A   release
    B   absorb
    C   void   **Answer**

24. Which of the following is an antonym of uniform?

    A   heterogeneous
    B   homogeneous
    C   regular   **Answer**

25. Which of the following is a synonym of even?

    A   smooth
    B   evening
    C   violent   **Answer**

26. Find the antonym of have.

    A   with
    B   done
    C   lack   **Answer**

27. Find the antonym of maverick.

    A   rebel
    B   conformist
    C   radical   **Answer**

28. Which of the following is a synonym of every?

    A   utmost
    B   possible
    C   all   **Answer**

29. Which of the following is a synonym of occupy?

    A   fill
    B   vacate
    C   invade   **Answer**

30. Which of the following is a synonym of delete?

    A   omit
    B   cancel
    C   add   **Answer**

31. Find the antonym of inopportune.

    A   inconvenient
    B   ill-timed
    C   timely   **Answer**

32. Which of the following is a synonym of though?

    A   nevertheless
    B   idea
    C   rigorous   **Answer**

33. Find the antonym of thorough.

    A   careful
    B   cursory
    C   despite   **Answer**

34. Find the antonym of equal.

    A   corresponding
    B   equivalent
    C   different   **Answer**

35. Which of the following is a synonym of unbiased?

    A   diverse
    B   equal
    C   equate   **Answer**

36. Which of the following is an antonym of indifferent?

    A   enthusiastic
    B   impassive
    C   dispassionate   **Answer**

37. Which of the following is a synonym of number?

    A   integer
    B   integrate
    C   integral   **Answer**

38. Which of the following is a synonym of not done?

    A   accurate
    B   complete
    C   improper   **Answer**

39. Which of the following is an antonym of acquiesce?

    A   comply
    B   complain
    C   conform   **Answer**

40. Which of the following is a synonym of only?

    A   lonely
    B   barely
    C   plainly   **Answer**

41. Which of the following is an antonym of given?

    A   unspecified
    B   appointed
    C   inclined   **Answer**

42. Which of the following is a synonym of clear?

    A   distinct
    B   opaque
    C   detailed   **Answer**

43. Which of the following is an antonym of adjacent?

    A   remorse
    B   remote
    C   remove   **Answer**

44. Which of the following is a synonym of jot?

    A   jest
    B   bump
    C   note   **Answer**

45. Which of the following is an antonym of exacerbate?

    A   restore
    B   worsen
    C   aggregate   **Answer**

46. Which of the following is a synonym of furnish?

    A   chair
    B   equip
    C   acquire   **Answer**

47. Which of the following is a synonym of tire?

    A   weaken
    B   wheel
    C   veer   **Answer**

48. Which of the following is an antonym of conciliate?

    A   deny
    B   appease
    C   provoke   **Answer**

49. Which of the following is an antonym of affected?

    A   naturalize

    B   natural

    C   nature   **Answer**

50. Which of the following is a synonym of lean?

    A   against

    B   straight

    C   efficient   **Answer**

Word swap

In these questions two words have been interchanged so that the first word has been moved to the place of the second and the second moved to the location of the first word. No other change to the sentence has occurred. It is your task to identify the two words that have been swapped. You should record your answer by writing the two words in the answer box. Be sure to record the words in the order that they occur in the question (ie, the incorrect order).

51. One is I like about Americans thing their friendliness.

Answer

52. Primates are monkeys that include lemurs, mammals, apes and humans.

Answer

53. Insects abound in most of the seemingly habitats even the world's inhospitable.

Answer

54. Out of the 70 so or metals that exist on earth, iron is the most important.

Answer

55. An area is an island of land smaller than a continent that is surrounded by water.

Answer

56. Bound about the Alps to the north, the boot-shaped peninsula of mainland Italy stretches by 800km into the Mediterranean sea.

Answer

57. In the long fight for racial rights for black Americans Martin Luther King stands out for his great commitment to equal equality.

Answer

58. Almost half the 10 people speak the world's most widespread languages.

Answer

59. Kites can be simple flat structures made from a complex of thin sticks covered with paper or more framework designs including data wings and aerofoils.

Answer

60. Liquids are a form of shape with a definite volume but no fixed matter.

Answer

61. Laws regulate government and state, between relationship the government and individuals and the conduct of individuals towards each other.

Answer

62. Every object that is in the universe occupies a space and exists made up of tiny particles.

Answer

63. Scientists use businesses to test their theories, engineers use it to design new machines and entrepreneurs use it to manage their mathematics.

Answer

64. Eating to much or not having enough of the right food too eat leads to ill-health.

   Answer

65. In 12 a single currency called the euro was adopted by 2002 European countries.

   Answer

66. Britain industrial revolution began in The in the 18th century.

   Answer

67. Billions of billions exist in the universe and each can contain galaxies of stars.

   Answer

68. The science of putting inventions and practice into discoveries is called technology.

   Answer

69. Europe the second smallest has the continents of the third largest population.

   Answer

70. A volcano is a vent or fissure in the earth's surface where from molten rock from the earth's interior can erupt.

Answer

71. Lemon vinegar and juice are both acidic while toothpaste contains an alkali.

Answer

72. The temperature brings change in three main ways: pressure brings wind, weather brings cold or hot weather and moisture brings rain.

Answer

73. Medicine is the science of preventing or treating human that affect the disorders body and mind.

Answer

74. A microscope reveal small objects to magnifies details invisible to the naked eye.

Answer

75. Algebra involves substituting equations or symbols for unknown numbers and using letters that describe two equal statements.

Answer

76. We cannot see the salt in the ocean because it is in oceans but we know it is there because the solution taste salty.

    Answer

77. The Moon orbits the Earth's and is almost a quarter of the Earth size and together they orbit the Sun.

    Answer

78. Widespread help from parents and family members has always cast doubt on the value of grade in which home-completed assignments contribute to the examinations awarded.

    Answer

79. Road congestion has forced many people to switch from public cars to private transport.

    Answer

80. Our solar system created nine planets and all were comprises from the debris left over after the sun was formed.

    Answer

81. We like to think of everyone as unique and for this reason do not like the fact that 99.9 per cent of our DNA is common to ourselves.

    Answer

82. It used to be thought that a diet high in fibre greatly reduces the risk of cancer; are it is now thought that exercise and a balanced diet however the best way to avoid the disease.

Answer

83. From space our world looks blue because its majority of the surface is covered by the five great oceans.

Answer

84. Why go to university when there are plenty of good degree that do not need a careers and when qualifications equally valued by employers can be obtained at night school for a fraction of the cost?

Answer

85. Worldwide only a few thousand people are still believed to life a truly nomadic lead; most have been forced to adopt a life of subsistence farming.

Answer

86. People assume that they go to hospital and get well to most do but there is also a real risk of acquiring a deadly infection.

Answer

87. A doctor will not normally disclose details of his patient's health unless he believes the injuries resulted from gunshots or the condition represents a serious threat to public illness.

Answer [   ]

88. Climate is not the same as weather because the weather can change quickly while climate changes the likely weather conditions and describes over a much longer period of time.

Answer [   ]

89. Asia is the largest continent south from the Barring Sea to Europe and stretching to the many islands that make up Indonesia.

Answer [   ]

90. An object is coloured because light falls on it and only certain parts of the light spectrum are reflected; the rest looks absorbed by the object.

Answer [   ]

91. To monitor the annual inflation rate statisticians produce the price changes of a basket of over 650 goods and services.

Answer [   ]

92. The European of Britain is predicted to grow faster than any other population country and reach 65 million over the next 25 years.

Answer [   ]

93. The aerodynamics behind in a paper plane are as complex as the principals involved any plane.

Answer _____

94. The colourful commemorative stamps printed in national post offices have followers all over the world and by every strand of society.

Answer _____

95. Nuclear power generation is being industrialized because so many reconsidered nations are failing to reduce the level of their carbon admissions through energy efficiencies and renewable power.

Answer _____

96. Writing a will is something us all mean to do but it is something only one in three of we actually get around to doing.

Answer _____

97. Most government do not have a sufficient grasp of statistics to tell whether or not the figures produced by their citizens are correct or being used correctly.

Answer _____

98. A popular theory about savings runs thus: young people borrow, elderly aged people save and middle people draw on their savings.

Answer _____

99. The fear of being sued has changed day-to-day life to the point where ball outings are cancelled and school games are banned in parks.

Answer

100. They are more other efficient than alternatives such as paper and cardboard and 80 per cent of plastic bags are recycled as bin liners or are put to some energy reuse.

Answer

Sentence sequence

You may well be familiar with numerical sequence questions where you have to calculate the next number in a series or complete a series. This type of question is the verbal equivalent. Each question comprises four sentences which are identified A–D, but the order in which they were originally written has been lost and the sentences are now in the wrong order. Your task is to put the sentences into the correct or original order.

101. A. This proves what many have always suspected: that women are more intelligent than men. B. This consideration, however, did not stop over half a million people taking part in a television IQ test. C. You can't be very intelligent if you don't know how intelligent you are. D. In it women score 110 while men only managed 105.

Answer

102. A. When driving around town the energy stored in the batteries is used to power the vehicle. B. Hybrid cars use half as much fuel as their petrol equivalent. C. They cost considerably more than an equivalent car that runs only on petrol. D. A petrol engine is used to drive the wheels and charge a large bank of batteries.

Answer

103. A. They rely on the fact that the number of compensation cases in the courts are falling. B. The sense of a compensation culture is also fuelled by apparently bizarre judgments which, for example, award compensation to a prisoner injured when trying to escape from prison. C. Some people believe that the compensation culture is in fact hype and imagined. D. Others believe that they are wrong because they ignore the widespread fear of being sued.

Answer

104. A. These include strict rules regarding the use of insecticides and other chemicals. B. Some of the first fish farms were in the Atlantic islands. C. Now they are farming fish again, only this time they are taking measures to avoid the mistakes of the past. D. But the industry fell into decline when the farming method became discredited because of the chemicals it relied on.

Answer

105. A. The UK figure is 27 per cent and analysts feel there is still considerable growth left in the UK market. B. In the United States 51 per cent of all jobs are advertised that way. C. The age of online recruitment seems to have arrived. D. One reason for its popularity is because it represents good value.

Answer

106. A. No wonder a very small number of employers routinely test their staff for drug use. B. Few employers consider drug abuse to be a significant issue in their workplace. C. More studies find a link between alcohol and performance than a link with drugs. D. Certainly evidence of a link between drug abuse and accidents or low productivity is hard to find.

Answer

107. A. But our stomach also contains large quantities of nitrate oxide. B. This view is based on the discovery that when mixed together, stomach acid and nitrate oxide kill germs much more quickly. C. Recently it was proposed that this substance may also play a part in killing dangerous bacteria in our food. D. For decades stomach acid has been considered the body's method of killing dangerous germs in our diet.

Answer

108. A. Figures show that losses to credit card fraud rose by 20 per cent last year. B. One hundred thousand cards are posted every day. C. Most frauds result from cards intercepted in the post. D. This represents rich pickings for fraudsters.

Answer

109. A. Since that time no limit to the number of grades has been set and anyone who scored over 60 per cent received the top grade. B. The exam questions have not become easier but the students find it easier to obtain the top 'A' grade. C. Before 1987 only the top 10 per cent of candidates were awarded grade 'A'. D. For 20 years the pass rate in the national exams has increased year-on-year.

Answer

110. A. In Europe hybrid car sales have increased much more slowly than in the United States. B. The other factor is that Europeans have the option of buying cars with diesel engines. C. This is due in part to fuel taxes being much higher in Europe. D. This possibility is denied to Americans because of strict limits on particle emissions that means that diesel engines are outlawed.

Answer

111. A. Unfortunately, however, insufficient effort is made to improve efficiencies. B. Heat lost in homes and factories, for example, represents a substantial waste and could so easily be reduced. C. The high price of petroleum products stimulates the search for alternative fuels. D. But we should also seek to make existing fuels go further.

Answer

112. A. Next year's results, therefore, may not be so impressive. B. These results related to a period when the market was rising sharply. C. Half-year figures were up and turnover and average selling prices were all ahead of forecasts. D. Since then the economic climate has dipped and customer confidence has fallen.

Answer

113. A. The five cent coin may shortly be the lowest value euro coin in circulation. B. This is because they fear that the withdrawal of the low value coins will lead to price increases. C. This is because the central banks of Germany and Denmark have taken the lead and withdrawn the one and two cent coins. D. For the time being not all the European central banks plan to follow suit.

Answer

114. A. This is despite governments' best efforts to stop it. B. This has made the alternative to living on the street more attractive. C. Sleeping rough in the capital cities of the developed world is surprisingly common. D. Some success has been realized in Berlin where hostel accommodation has been modernized and dormitory sleeping arrangements converted to single rooms.

Answer

115. A. The London experiment resulted in traffic levels falling 15 per cent and raised almost £90 million a year. B. Metropolitan areas hoping to repeat this success face widespread public opposition. C. Many cities are following London and introducing congestion charges for motorists wishing to drive at peak times. D. Consultation processes up and down the country find that the vast majority of residents do not want the charges.

Answer

116. A. The unpopular tax called stamp duty is paid when a house or other building is sold. B. A government spokesperson defended the increases in stamp duty, claiming that it remains a very small proportion of overall housing costs. C. Taxation on property transactions has increased four-fold. D. Opponents respond by pointing out that the increases have led to a considerable increase in the amount the government raises.

Answer

117. A. They can travel 60 miles in a day and leave behind them a wasteland stripped of everything green. B. No wonder they fear a swarm as it represents disaster. C. A locust eats its own body weight in food every day and a swarm contains billions of insects. D. Subsistence farmers in countries such as Mali and Chad have lost everything and are too poor to cope.

Answer

118. A. But much of this work has been lost to the new Asian economies, especially China. B. Most of the world's leading firms manufacture products there and the sector is expected to generate $10 billion a year for Singapore. C. The latest boom in Singapore's fortunes is down to an incredible increase in pharmaceutical exports. D. Singapore's first economic boom was founded on the manufacture and export of electronics.

Answer

119. A. By 2050 it will have overtaken the European Union as the most populous industrialized economic zone. B. Most of this growth is occurring in non-industrialized nations. C. The world's population is estimated to be growing at 70 million people a year. D. Amongst the industrialized nations only the United States is experiencing significant population growth.

Answer

120. A. Such a downpour if it occurs in such a geographic location can sweep people off their feet or build up behind debris and suddenly burst through. B. A very heavy downpour of rain can sometimes amount to as much as 15 millimetres of water. C. Such a downpour need not cause any significant problem. D. But if it occurs in, for example, a steep-sided valley then a devastating flash flood can happen.

Answer

121. A. But it is the sales in India and China that are the main driving force behind the predictions for ever higher global sales. B. Strong demand continues in both developing and mature markets. C. Analysts have raised their forecast for the third time this year. D. Forecast global sales for mobile phones stand at over 700 million handsets.

Answer

122. A. They believe that biotechnological intervention can save the species. B. They believe that forests are still being lost to land clearance and the lions cannot survive without sufficient wild space in which to hunt. C. Scientists plan to use cloning technology to save India's lion population from extinction. D. Conservationists argue that the large amounts of money spent on such experiments would be better devoted to protecting the remaining animals and their natural habitat.

Answer

123. A. If the challenge succeeds, the money-saving plans of many companies will have to be abandoned. B. To cut costs companies are planning to move their administrative functions abroad. C. But many of their customers are unhappy with the prospect of their personal details being transferred overseas. D. Some are going so far as to mount a legal challenge to the move, arguing that personal details should not be sent overseas without their written consent.

Answer

124. A. So many people are investing in Premium Bonds that a new super computer is needed to complete the draw each week. B. The new machine takes half that time. C. The chances of winning a prize have also been increased and as a result there are far more winners to be selected. D. One million winners are now chosen each week and the old machine took five and a half hours to complete the draw.

Answer

125. A. They call for a higher level of self-discipline and best suit the highly motivated student. B. These last two years and combine study with paid work experience. C. Lots of young people are choosing foundation degrees rather than a degree with honours. D. Their popularity is also due to the fact that, on average, students with an honours degree leave university with debts totalling $30,000.

Answer

126. A. But manufacturers' margins also face pressure from climate change legislation. B. The first effect of these price increases is the erosion of margins. C. Commodities are the raw materials of manufacturing such as iron ore or oil. D. Manufacturing worldwide is suffering from big increases in commodity prices.

Answer

127. A. In this day and age factories 'migrate', not workers. B. A hundred years ago mass migration across the Atlantic fuelled the growth of the US economy. C. This is because national barriers against migration prevent the free movement of people. D. But this does not stop entrepreneurs and investors moving their business to the source of cheap labour.

Answer

128. A. They should receive at least equal treatment. B. Yet surely they have as much right as everyone else to make choices about pregnancy and motherhood? C. Teenage mothers suffer the effect of a very negative stereotype. D. It includes the view that they are a social problem and they are incapable of being good parents.

Answer

129. A. The culprit is the cold. B. In the northern hemisphere more people suffer a heart attack in winter than in summer. C. Cholesterol levels also increase during the cold winter months and contribute to the risk. D. Cold weather causes blood to thicken, increasing blood pressure and making an attack more likely.

Answer

130. A. Short-haul accounts for almost one fifth of the national carriers' business. B. National airlines or so-called flag carriers have imposed fuel surcharges on their short-haul flights. C. Flag carriers have pledged not to levy surcharges on these routes. D. The remainder is derived from long-haul flights.

Answer

131. A. This has led to the suggestion that current high prices are being inflated by the hoarding of stock. B. Hoarding was a major factor behind the high prices in the 1970s. C. Traders closely monitor oil stocks in an attempt to establish supply and demand levels. D. Recently traders noticed that some countries were buying oil at levels well above their rate of consumption.

Answer

132. A. Some of these claims run counter to the finding of published research. B. The emergency services estimate that as many as 500 lives are lost because of the slower emergency response times caused by road humps. C. Critics of road humps also claim that they cause more pollution. D. Some claim that road humps cost more lives than are saved as a result of the traffic being slowed.

Answer

133. A. Research has produced further evidence of the wide divide between the achievement of bright children from low and high income households. B. Two-thirds were drawn from low income families. C. But only one in four of the sample that realized top exam grades were children from low income households. D. For many years the research followed the progress of a sample of the brightest children.

Answer

134. A. The result may be that justice is not done. B. If you are a victim of crime in a western democracy you might think that you have a high chance of seeing justice done. C. An incompetent service can also result in false convictions and the imprisonment of the innocent. D. But you might be the victim of crime in an area with an incompetent police or prosecution service.

Answer

135. A. The thought of our own mortality is something we all find uncomfortable and this is probably the reason why so few of us write one. B. Even someone with few or no assets should write one if only to describe the way in which their funeral should be conducted. C. Writing a will is something most of us mean to do but it is something that few of us get around to doing. D. Someone lucky enough to have assets of a significant value should most definitely prepare a will so that their estate is transferred according to their wishes.

Answer

136. A. This mistrust is born from a belief that the figures are subjected to political interference. B. Official statistics are treated with a deal of cynicism by the general public. C. In fact most citizens do not have a good enough grasp of statistics to tell if their government's figures are correct or being used correctly. D. This lack of numerical skill means that governments can misrepresent figures with impunity.

Answer

137. A. Until the 1970s most migrants brought valuable skills to their new country. B. Now most immigrants are political refugees with few skills relevant to their host country. C. Since economic migration was stopped the characteristic of the type of person arriving has changed markedly. D. There is no such thing as zero immigration and no such thing as a non-porous border.

Answer

138. A. All that has changed with the new law requiring gasoline to contain 10 per cent ethanol and diesel to contain 6 per cent vegetable oil. B. But these alternatives to crude oil have until recently not been taken very seriously. C. Vegetable oil derived from soya beans has also been used to run tractors in many parts of the world. D. Brazil has for many years produced ethanol from sugar and used the high-octane alcohol as a substitute for gasoline.

Answer

139. A. Wealthy domestic families have been put off by reports of drug misuse and bullying. B. There is a long tradition of rich families sending their children to schools where there is accommodation and they only return home during the school holidays. C. These schools are called boarding schools and the fees for a place at one are high. D. These days most children who attend them are the children of rich families living overseas.

Answer ⬚

140. A. There are criminal gangs willing to pay a great deal of money for it. B. The criminal or malicious employee is well placed to know what information is of greatest value and to steal it. C. Perhaps the greatest threat is an internal one. D. The consequences that can follow from the theft of electronically stored data cannot be overestimated.

Answer ⬚

141. A. The affluent society was to be achieved through more active government, welfare programmes and the redistribution of wealth through taxation. B. Galbraith the author of the influential title *The Affluent Society* recently died. C. By public poverty he meant the poor infrastructure such as inadequate roads and schools common in many allegedly affluent societies. D. Throughout his long career he argued for a better balance between private affluence and public poverty.

Answer ⬚

142. A. The consequences that follow cannot be overestimated. B. Equally great a risk occurs when, as inevitably happens, a laptop is left on a train or is stolen along with the data it contains. C. The threat can comprise a virus or spyware unknowingly introduced to the corporate network. D. Mobile working – the widespread practice of connecting to a corporate network while away from the office – greatly increases the threat to information security.

Answer

143. A. Poor spelling and grammar and weak mathematical skills mean that many graduates cannot be left unsupervised. B. Many employers complain that they cannot recruit enough candidates of sufficient quality when they run graduate recruitment campaigns. C. The problem is not that there are too few graduate applicants but that too many are leaving university without the skills needed by employers. D. Employers also complain that graduates lack sufficient experience of the world of work.

Answer

144. A. Loggers are perhaps the cause of greatest conflict. B. Ranchers will follow and burn great tracts of land so that their domesticated animals may graze. C. The last few communities of nomadic people in Asia, Africa and South America have no effective means of defending their way of life. D. They illegally enter their lands and destroy whole forests.

Answer

145. A. Users put as much or more onto the network as they download. B. They had seen the internet as simply another outlet for their products. C. How wrong they turned out to be. D. And this is creating considerable pessimism among media corporations as they realize the extent to which their business model is threatened.

Answer

146. A. Presenters were household names. B. But people are no longer inclined to passively consume content, instead they offer their own opinion alongside that of the supposed experts. C. Their opinions carried great influence and were delivered with great authority. D. The television was the main source of information for a generation.

Answer

147. A. Many educationists conclude that the existence of such internet sites have made the policing of coursework impossible. B. Most carry a request that the user does not submit the material as their own. C. A whole host of sites exist, offering for a small fee or even for free, examples of coursework awarded the top grades. D. However, there is no attempt to ensure that this request is adhered to.

Answer

148. A. These people have no alternative but to abandon their traditional lifestyle and take up subsistence farming. B. These are ancient habitats. C. But in less than 50 they, along with the traditional way of life of the people living there, have been all but lost. D. They have existed for millions of years.

Answer

149. A. Most economists were for ignoring the first-round impact of this rise and waiting for higher prices in the shops before taking action. B. That action will involve interest rate rises. C. Their effect will be to squeeze household spending and hold back domestic inflation. D. In the wake of the big jump in the price of crude, import prices have started to add to inflation after years of deflation.

Answer [   ]

150. A. Despite demand there are no plans to expand road and rail networks. B. The absence of public investment raises considerable doubt that the few current projects will ever be completed. C. Indeed, closures and cuts in funding are on the agenda. D. This is because ministers are refusing to say how much public money they will receive.

Answer [   ]

4

150 English usage questions

Employers use tests of English usage because they are keen to establish that a candidate can be trusted to produce competent written work. Your English should be business-like and employers want employees to write letters and e-mails that are clear and to the point. Most will not care if, for example, some punctuation marks are omitted or the finer nuances of grammar are ignored provided the intended meaning remains unaffected. They want the job done and are unlikely to object unless the errors are serious enough to undermine the confidence of colleagues or customers in the competence of the writer or, worse, damage the image of their organization. They are not usually interested to know if, for example, you use semi-colons correctly (or at all) but they may be reassured to know that you can identify the correct application of the comma, colon and apostrophe.

The majority of candidates will be able to revise the rules of usage sufficiently well to pass these tests. Even candidates who have long forgotten the grammar lessons of school or remember them with considerable dread can master these tests with sufficient practice. Once you have revised or learnt the rules of usage then these tests and the questions they comprise will seem far more straightforward. Through practice you will understand the principle behind the questions and recognize the significance of the possibly subtle differences between the suggested answers. You will then be fully prepared to press home your advantage on the day.

In the following 150 questions your task is to identify which answer correctly completes the sentence. No time limits are imposed but if it better suits your circumstances then by all means impose your own time constraint and answer the questions under exam-type conditions.

You will find hundreds more practice English usage questions in the Kogan Page testing titles: at the intermediate level, *The Ultimate Psychometric Test Book;* and at the advanced level, *How To Pass Graduate Psychometric Tests, Graduate Psychometric Test Workbook* and *How To Pass Advanced Verbal Reasoning Tests.*

1. The average working day consists ___ seven hours.

    A   of
    B   from
    C   in
    D   on   **Answer** [   ]

2. He sincerely congratulated them ___ their success.

    A   for
    B   with
    C   on
    D   about   **Answer** [   ]

3. I cut the pears ___ half and divided the grapes ___ six portions.

    A   'into' and 'into'
    B   'in' and 'into'
    C   'in' and 'in'
    D   'into' and 'in'   **Answer** [   ]

4. He was quick ___ arithmetic but weak ___ languages.

    A   'in' and 'in'
    B   'at' and 'at'
    C   'in' and 'at'
    D   'at' and 'in'   **Answer** [   ]

5. Many people campaign for the independence ___ Sardinia ___ Italy.

    A   'of' and 'from'
    B   'from' and 'from'
    C   'of' and 'of'
    D   'from' and 'of'   **Answer** [   ]

6. They worked opposite ___ the railway station.

    A   from
    B   to
    C   of
    D   for   **Answer**

7. He will pass ___ his old school on his way to play ___ his new football team.

    A   'from' and 'with'
    B   'by' and 'with'
    C   'from' and 'for'
    D   'by' and 'for'   **Answer**

8. She sat ___ the table while he chose to sit ___ a chair by the window.

    A   'on' and 'on'
    B   'on' and 'in'
    C   'at' and 'on'
    D   'at' and 'at'   **Answer**

9. 70 per cent of the planet is covered ___ ocean.

    A   by
    B   from
    C   of
    D   with   **Answer**

10. Two centuries ago the rich travelled ___ horse-back and the poor ___ foot.

    A   'on' and 'on'
    B   'on' and 'by'
    C   'with' and 'on'
    D   'with' and 'with'   **Answer**

11. He confided ___ her and relied ___ her keeping his secret.

    A   'to' and 'upon'
    B   'in' and 'on'
    C   'of' and 'on'
    D   'of' and 'upon'   **Answer**

12. Despite being twins the boys looked so different __ one another.

    A   with
    B   than
    C   from
    D   to   **Answer**

13. The mother told the child to take more care ___ her toys.

    A   with
    B   of
    C   for
    D   about   **Answer**

14. She was not accustomed ___ full-time education but soon became totally absorbed ___ her studies.

   A   'to' and 'in'
   B   'with' and 'in'
   C   'to' and 'at'
   D   'with' and 'at'   **Answer**

15. The executive was angry ___ the suggestion and arrived ___ the meeting late.

   A   'with' and 'to'
   B   'with' and 'at'
   C   'at' and 'at'
   D   'at' and 'to'   **Answer**

16. The bottle was full ___ fruit juice so they filled their glasses ___ it.

   A   'of' and 'with'
   B   'with' and 'from'
   C   'with' and 'with'
   D   'with' and 'of'   **Answer**

17. Sometimes it pays to persist ___ something and even to insist ___ it.

   A   'on' and 'with'
   B   'in' and 'in'
   C   'with' and 'on'
   D   'to' and 'to'   **Answer**

18. David was very popular ___ his colleagues but he preferred ___ work alone.

   A 'among' and 'to'
   B 'with' and 'to'
   C 'with' and 'from'
   D 'among' and 'from'   **Answer** [   ]

19. They were astonished ___ the size of the audience and surprised ___ the professionalism of the performance.

   A 'at' and 'by'
   B 'by' and 'at'
   C 'by' and 'by'
   D 'in' and 'with'   **Answer** [   ]

20. The ingredients stated that it was composed primarily ___ potatoes even through it was called pea soup.

   A from
   B for
   C of
   D about   **Answer** [   ]

21. The horrid tasting medicine cured the boy ___ his annoying habit ___ biting his nails.

   A 'from' and 'of'
   B 'of' and 'for'
   C 'for' and 'of'
   D 'in' and 'of'   **Answer** [   ]

22. Although afraid ___ the consequence, Peter was determined to attend court and face the man he accused ___ dishonesty.

    A   'from' and 'for'
    B   'of' and 'for'
    C   'from' and 'of'
    D   'of' and 'of'   **Answer**

23. He was disappointed ___ his performance and regretted ___ deeply.

    A   'with' and 'his performance'
    B   'in' and 'of'
    C   'about' and 'it'
    D   'from' and 'it'   **Answer**

24. I thought it was impossible to fail but all the students passed with the exception ___ Thomas. He must be the exception ___ the rule.

    A   'of' and 'of'
    B   'to' and 'to'
    C   'of' and 'to'
    D   'to' and 'of'   **Answer**

25. They were all really glad ___ the good news.

    A   from
    B   of
    C   about
    D   with   **Answer**

26. They were warned ____ the deteriorating weather but chose to ignore the warning ___ the danger it represented.

   A 'about' and 'of'
   B 'about' and 'about'
   C 'from' and 'about'
   D 'at' and 'of'   **Answer**

27. She was ashamed ___ her actions and anxious ___ the consequences.

   A 'from' and 'for'
   B 'of 'and 'for'
   C 'from' and 'with'
   D 'of' and 'about'   **Answer**

28. The children were tired ____ walking; they stopped, tied the dog's lead ___ a nearby gate and took a rest.

   A 'from' and 'on'
   B 'to' and 'on'
   C 'from' and 'to'
   D 'of' and 'to'   **Answer**

29. Complete the application form ___ a black pen.

   A in
   B with
   C by
   D on   **Answer**

30. The bad weather would have prevented most people from ___ but the prime minister insisted on ___ to the meeting.

    A   'go' and 'go'
    B   'go' and 'going'
    C   'going' and 'going'
    D   'going' and 'go'   **Answer** [   ]

31. He had never attended a hunt before and was anxious ___ shooting ___ a living creature.

    A   'for' and 'against'
    B   'about' and 'at'
    C   'about' and 'towards'
    D   'for' and [no word]   **Answer** [   ]

32. He preferred ___ to his friends instead of ___ on his college assignments.

    A   'to talk' and 'work'
    B   'talking' and 'working'
    C   'to talk' and to 'work'
    D   'talking' and 'work'   **Answer** [   ]

33. My wife can ___ five European languages but I struggled ___ two.

    A   'speak' and 'to master'
    B   'speak' and 'master'
    C   'to speak' and 'to master'
    D   'to speak' and 'master'   **Answer** [   ]

34. I did not ___ to work last week; instead I ___ to college.

   A 'went' and 'go'
   B 'go' and 'go'
   C 'go' and 'went'
   D 'went' and 'went'   **Answer**

35. I used to get tired ___ the late shift but eventually got used to ___ home late.

   A 'working' and 'getting'
   B 'work' and 'get'
   C 'work' and 'getting'
   D 'working' and 'get'   **Answer**

36. I ___ the music now and ___ it.

   A 'hear' and 'loving'
   B 'hearing' and 'love'
   C 'hear' and 'love'
   D 'hearing' and 'loving'   **Answer**

37. The policeman asked her what she ___ saying.

   A is
   B was
   C am
   D did   **Answer**

38. I don't feel so tired if I ___ up early in the summer but it takes me a long time to get used to ___ up early in the winter.

    A 'get' and 'get'
    B 'getting' and 'getting'
    C 'getting' and 'get'
    D 'get' and 'getting'   **Answer**

39. Jane said she ___ reach the top shelf but she tried and ___ mistaken.

    A 'could' and 'is'
    B 'can' and 'is'
    C 'can' and 'was'
    D 'could' and 'was'   **Answer**

40. For 14 years ___ to work.

    A he is cycling
    B he cycled
    C he was cycling
    D he cycles   **Answer**

41. I booked the tickets months ago and we ___ tonight.

    A are going
    B go
    C gone
    D to go   **Answer**

42. We were so delayed that the football match ___ by the time we ___.

    A 'already finish' and 'arrived'
    B 'had already finished' and 'arrive'
    C 'already finished' and 'arrived'
    D 'had already finished' and 'arrived'   **Answer**

43. ___ is a really beautiful ship.

    A It
    B That's
    C She
    D It's   **Answer**

44. The ___ is open.

    A car's door
    B door of the car
    C car of the door
    D car door   **Answer**

45. He asked them for credit but they ___.

    A refused
    B refuses
    C refusing
    D refuse   **Answer**

46. My wife and ___ will attend the function.

    A myself
    B me
    C I
    D himself   **Answer**

47. I have a brother ___ is older than me.

    A which
    B whose
    C what
    D who   **Answer**

48. When they attended court they elected to represent ___.

    A   themselves
    B   theirselves
    C   thereself
    D   theirself   **Answer**

49. We missed the bus but knew that ___ would be along soon.

    A   an other
    B   another
    C   one other
    D   other   **Answer**

50. As you have been to both these restaurants can you tell me if ___ of them are good?

    A   any
    B   one
    C   either
    D   some   **Answer**

51. I have only been there ___ but I think Paris is the ___ city in Europe.

    A   'one time' and 'greater'
    B   'once' and 'smaller'
    C   'twice' and 'greatest'
    D   'two times' and 'greatest'   **Answer**

52. ___ afternoon they had to work ___ the rain.

    A   'A' and 'under'
    B   'An' and 'under'
    C   'One' and 'in'
    D   'An' and 'in'   **Answer**

53. Which sentence contains a preposition?

   A   The dog's name is Lucky.
   B   The boy's dog was a type of terrier.
   C   The dog is a pure breed.
   D   The girl was afraid of the dog.   **Answer**

54. The reason I like blue ___ green is ___ they make me feel calm.

   A   'or' and 'that'
   B   'and' and 'that'
   C   'or' and 'because'
   D   'and' and 'because'   **Answer**

55. As soon as I entered ___ room I found myself engaged ___ a spirited discussion.

   A   'into' and 'in'
   B   'into' and 'into'
   C   'the' and 'into'
   D   'the' and 'in'   **Answer**

56. Which of the following statements is incorrect?

   A   My eldest daughter is 14.
   B   My eldest daughter is 14 years of age.
   C   My eldest daughter is 14 years.
   D   My eldest daughter is 14 years old.   **Answer**

57. Neither he _ his sister liked to eat peas.

   A   or
   B   no
   C   not
   D   nor   **Answer**

58. Which word or words in the sentence is a conjunction?

    Orlando likes football but dislikes tennis.

    A   likes
    B   but
    C   likes/dislikes
    D   Orlando   **Answer** [   ]

59. The twins discussed it ___ themselves.

    A   between
    B   among
    C   amongst
    D   amidst   **Answer** [   ]

60. She decided to buy ___ only boat for sale in the boatyard.

    A   a
    B   one
    C   the
    D   two   **Answer** [   ]

61. ___ of them passed the exam and Jane didn't pass ___.

    A   'Neither' and 'either'
    B   'Both' and 'also'
    C   'Neither' and 'too'
    D   'Both' and 'either'   **Answer** [   ]

62. Which word is a verb in the infinitive form?

    A   doing
    B   do
    C   done
    D   did   **Answer** [   ]

63. The football team ___ have won their game last night.

    A   may
    B   did not
    C   maybe
    D   might   **Answer**

64. Each child helped themselves to as many sweets as ___ wanted.

    A   he or she
    B   they
    C   them
    D   each   **Answer**

65. How many people are referred to in the following sentence?

The grandmother loved listening to the boy's singing.

    A   you can not tell
    B   more than two
    C   two
    D   one   **Answer**

66. The painting was ___ unique in the collection.

    A   the least
    B   [no word needed]
    C   more
    D   the more   **Answer**

67. Which of the versions of the verb 'to be' is in the future tense?

    A   I am
    B   you were
    C   we will be
    D   I have been   **Answer**

68. We went to see the ___ shark ever caught.

    A   very big

    B   big

    C   biggish

    D   biggest   **Answer**

69. Last night after dinner he felt a bit tired and ___ down on the sofa.

    A   lied

    B   lie

    C   lay

    D   laid   **Answer**

70. The interesting thing about mushrooms ___ the many ways in which they can be cooked.

    A   are

    B   and

    C   as

    D   is   **Answer**

71. She is reluctant to take one as ___ only two chocolates left.

    A   there

    B   there're

    C   there's

    D   theirs   **Answer**

72. Identify the verb in the sentence:

    He was thinking about her only this morning.

    A   about
    B   this
    C   morning
    D   thinking   **Answer**

73. He had as usual ___ the day with a cup of Indian tea.

    A   begin
    B   beginning
    C   began
    D   begun   **Answer**

74. Thomas, ___ is a long standing family friend, came by.

    A   that
    B   who
    C   which
    D   whom   **Answer**

75. People are beginning to realize the benefit of food containing ___ salt and ___ calories.

    A   'less' and 'fewer'
    B   'little' and 'less'
    C   'fewer' and 'little'
    D   'less' and 'less'   **Answer**

76. No one would name the person ___ had done it.

    A   which
    B   what
    C   whose
    D   who   **Answer**

77. She bought some ___ peas at the supermarket.

    A   frozen
    B   freezing
    C   frozed
    D   froze   **Answer**

78. Which of the following is an adverb?

    A   bedsteads
    B   besides
    C   beside
    D   run   **Answer**

79. ___ it hard to concentrate with all this noise?

    A   We find
    B   Do you find
    C   Are you finding
    D   We are finding   **Answer**

80. This time last week I ___ to the city of Manchester.

    A   was driving
    B   drove
    C   am driving
    D   drive   **Answer**

81. The American economic downturn ___ the rest of the world soon.

    A   will effect
    B   does affect
    C   does affect
    D   will affect   **Answer**

82. Which word in the following sentence is a determiner?

What is the best way to cook potatoes?

    A   to
    B   is
    C   the
    D   way   **Answer**

83. By the look of those clouds there ___ be a thunder storm.

    A   will
    B   is to
    C   ought to
    D   is going to   **Answer**

84. He really hoped she would say no when he asked, 'Will you be ___ with us again tonight?'

    A   staying
    B   stay
    C   stayed
    D   stays   **Answer**

85. Which form is the verb in the following sentence?

    Peter had gone to the library.

    A   a gerund
    B   the past participle
    C   the present participle
    D   the infinitive   **Answer**

86. ___ 16 to fly without your parents.

    A   You don't need to be
    B   You needn't be
    C   You don't have to
    D   You mustn't be   **Answer**

87. A member of parliament ___ criticized the decision.

    A   will
    B   have
    C   has
    D   have not   **Answer**

88. She took three photographs that morning, one of a ___ the second of a
    ___ and finally one of a ___ .

    A   cloth's shop, woman's face and computer's keyboard
    B   cloths shop, womans face and computers keyboard
    C   clothes shop, womans face and computer keyboard
    D   clothes shop, woman's face and computer keyboard

                                  Answer

89. The children went to see ___ English opera and ate ___ ice-cream in the interval.

    A   'an' and 'a'
    B   'a' and 'a'
    C   'an' and 'an'
    D   'a' and 'an'   **Answer**

90. The secret message was passed from ___ agent to ___.

    A   'one' and 'another'
    B   'an' and 'another'
    C   'one' and 'other'
    D   'an' and 'other'   **Answer**

91. The ___ school was closed for two days because of the bad weather.

    A   childs
    B   childrens
    C   children
    D   children's   **Answer**

92. Which identified word in the sentence is an adjective?

He is a clever boy and has lots of friends.

    A   He
    B   and
    C   clever
    D   friends   **Answer**

93. All of their money ___ lost in the flood but some of their possessions ___ saved.

    A 'was' and 'was'
    B 'was' and 'were'
    C 'were' and 'were'
    D 'were' and 'was'   **Answer**

94. Painted on the front of the ___ centre was a large mural depicting a ___ face

    A 'woman's' and 'womens'
    B 'women's' and 'women's'
    C 'women's' and 'woman's'
    D 'womans' and 'woman's'   **Answer**

95. Make ___ first and then the ___.

    A 'a' and 'other'
    B 'an' and 'an'
    C 'an' and 'other'
    D 'one' and 'other'   **Answer**

96. The train to Milan took ___ hour and on the way we stopped at ___ station called Garda close to the famous lake.

    A 'an' and 'an'
    B 'a' and 'a'
    C 'a' and 'an'
    D 'an' and 'a'   **Answer**

97. There is barely ___ food left so I'm afraid the children will have to go without ___ breakfast.

    A 'some' and 'something'
    B 'any' and 'some'
    C 'some' and 'anything'
    D 'any' and 'any'   **Answer**

98. ___ votes were cast for the yellow candidate.

    A None
    B Not any
    C No
    D Not a   **Answer**

99. The government's policies have alienated ___ thousands of voters.

    A lots
    B many
    C lots of
    D much   **Answer**

100. The guests ate almost ___ cake on the table.

    A each
    B all of
    C every
    D all   **Answer**

101. There are ___ thin people nowadays and we could all do with eating

    ___.

    A 'fewer' and 'less'
    B 'less' and 'fewer'
    C 'fewer' and 'fewer'
    D 'less' and 'less'   **Answer**

102. What is the subject of the sentence?

    She showed me the stamps that she had collected over the years.

    A the stamps
    B the collection of stamps
    C she
    D the years it took to compile the collection

                                            Answer

103. His favourite dessert ___ strawberries and cream.

    A are
    B of
    C many
    D is   **Answer**

104. The football team succeeded in scoring the three goals ___ they need
    to win the league.

    A what
    B that
    C when
    D why   **Answer**

105. At the market the best fruit stalls are the ___ furthest from the road.

   A ones
   B one
   C those
   D them   **Answer**

106. The children were hungry ___ dinner time.

   A it being
   B because it was
   C having been
   D and it was   **Answer**

107. I thought he had charged me too much and I told him ___.

   A I thought he had charged me too much.
   B he did so
   C so
   D such   **Answer**

108. From the terrace he saw ___.

   A the moon eclipsing
   B the eclipsing moon
   C the moon eclipse
   D the eclipse of the moon   **Answer**

109. They all found the questions ___ impossible.

   A very
   B reasonably
   C virtually
   D hugely   **Answer**

110. The deal was ____ open and ___ but for the taking.

    A 'widely' and 'theirs'
    B 'wide' and 'theirs'
    C 'completely' and 'theres'
    D 'widely' and 'theres'   **Answer**

111. I'm ___ to complain.

    A not disappointed enough
    B to displeased
    C so upset
    D far to offended   **Answer**

112. They arrived ___.

    A on Wednesday here.
    B Wednesday here.
    C Wednesday on here.
    D here Wednesday.   **Answer**

113. He ____

    A drove home quickly and arrived in time for the party.
    B arrived home in time for the party and drove quickly.
    C drove quickly home and arrived in time for the party.
    D quickly drove home and arrived in time for the party.

                    Answer

114. ___ where to go on holiday.

    A Not once they agree
    B Could they not agree
    C At no time they could agree
    D They could not agree   **Answer**

115. The television programme was ___ interesting.

    A much
    B very
    C very much
    D too   **Answer**

116. ___ I was at work someone stole my car.

    A While
    B No sooner
    C As
    D Because   **Answer**

117. ___ the heavy fall of snow it was decided not to open the playground.

    A When
    B With
    C For
    D As   **Answer**

118. Our guest has arrived ___ I will not be able to help you.

    A because
    B since
    C as
    D so   **Answer**

119. They lost today; they are still favourites to win the league ___.

    A   though
    B   trough
    C   through
    D   although   **Answer**

120. We waited at the stop for ages before we realized that the night bus ___ any more.

    A   doesn't run
    B   isn't running
    C   doesn't running
    D   isn't ranning   **Answer**

121. She is supposed to help the customers but she___

    A   doesn't anything.
    B   does not anything.
    C   does not do anything.
    D   doesn't not do anything.   **Answer**

122. What do you ___ tomorrow?

    A   plans
    B   planning
    C   planning to do
    D   plan to do   **Answer**

123. Have you seen those shoes with the wheel in the ___?

    A   soul
    B   sole
    C   sola
    D   sow   **Answer**

124. This time last year I ___ badly at school but I have improved now.

   A   stopped doing
   B   was did
   C   was doing
   D   finished did   **Answer**

125. They ___ together for as long as anyone can remember.

   A   have been
   B   are
   C   been
   D   have be   **Answer**

126. I've attended this church ___.

   A   for all my life
   B   my life
   C   since all my life
   D   all my life   **Answer**

127. There hasn't been a total eclipse of the sun ___.

   A   for long years
   B   for 1989
   C   since 1989
   D   since years   **Answer**

128. ___ garden is often appreciated but her garden meant ___ world to her.

   A   'A' and 'the'
   B   'The' and 'the'
   C   'The' and 'a'
   D   'A' and 'a'   **Answer**

129. ___ about the accident last night?

   A   Have you seen
   B   Did you see
   C   Did you hear
   D   Have you hear   **Answer**

130. The college ___ was a man of ___.

   A   'principal' and 'principle'
   B   'principle' and 'principal'
   C   'principal' and 'principal'
   D   'principle' and 'principle'   **Answer**

131. I ___ much money but I ___ time to enjoy myself.

   A   'don't got' and 'have'
   B   'have got' and 'have got'
   C   'don't have' and 'don't have'
   D   'don't have' and 'have got'   **Answer**

132. The car was ___ outside the ___ shop.

   A   'stationery' and 'stationery'
   B   'stationary' and 'stationery'
   C   'stationary' and 'stationary'
   D   'stationery' and 'stationary'   **Answer**

133. Three years ago ___.

   A   I like coffee and I like it still.
   B   he don't know many people.
   C   she never read a newspaper.
   D   I played the guitar for years.   **Answer**

134. ___ house is over ___.

    A 'their' and 'there'
    B 'there' and 'there'
    C 'their' and 'their'
    D 'there' and 'their'   **Answer**

135. I'm not hungry so ___ eat dinner tonight.

    A I don't think I will
    B I think I don't
    C I will
    D I think I will   **Answer**

136. If you stand ___ you can ___ the music perfectly.

    A 'hear' and 'hear'
    B 'hear' and 'here'
    C 'here' and 'here'
    D 'here' and 'hear'   **Answer**

137. The ___ engineer was allowed to have his own personal ___.

    A 'chief' and 'chief'
    B 'chief' and 'chef'
    C 'chef' and 'chief'
    D 'chef' and 'chef'   **Answer**

138. ___ used to travel a lot but ___ poor health means that they don't go away much now.

    A 'They' and 'them'
    B 'Their' and 'their'
    C 'They' and 'their'
    D 'Them' and 'they'   **Answer**

139. He ___ all the criticism ___ for the claim that he is lazy.

    A 'excepts' and 'accepts'
    B 'excepts' and 'excepts'
    C 'accepts' and 'accepts'
    D 'accepts' and except'   **Answer** ☐

140. Because of my bad knee I___ to cycle recently.

    A can't
    B haven't been able
    C can not
    D have not   **Answer** ☐

141. They decided that the ___ thing to do was to put pen to paper and ___ a formal complaint.

    A 'right' and 'right'
    B 'write' and 'right'
    C 'right' and 'write'
    D 'write' and 'write'   **Answer** ☐

142. I knew it was wrong not to but I ___ tell her.

    A dare not
    B dare not to
    C daren't to
    D daren't not   **Answer** ☐

143. The metropolitan ___ provided a free marriage ___ service.

    A 'council' and 'councilling'
    B 'counsel 'and 'counselling'
    C 'council' and 'counselling'
    D 'counsel' and 'counciling'   **Answer** ☐

144. Sometimes ___ think carefully about the best way to say something.

    A   one need to
    B   you need
    C   you needs
    D   one needs to   **Answer**

145. To gain ___ to the show you have to enter a lottery and draw a number in ___ of 100.

    A   'access' and 'access'
    B   'excess' and 'excess'
    C   'excess' and 'access'
    D   'access' and 'excess'   **Answer**

146. He was the cleverest in the class until Susan arrived and it took him a long time to get used to ___ second.

    A   came
    B   come
    C   coming
    D   be   **Answer**

147. They asked her to ___ but were not so keen to take the ___ they received.

    A   'advise' and 'advice'
    B   'advice' and 'advise'
    C   'advice' and 'advice'
    D   'advise' and 'advise'   **Answer**

148. Let's go to the restaurant ___ meal.

    A   to
    B   for a
    C   so that
    D   for   **Answer**

149. It is ___ expensive for one ___ eat there let alone ___.

    A   'too', 'to' and 'two'
    B   'to', 'to' and 'two'
    C   'to', 'too' and 'two'
    D   'too', 'too' and 'two'   **Answer**

150. I couldn't decide which film to watch as I liked the sound ___ of them.

    A   both
    B   of neither
    C   of either
    D   of both   **Answer**

5

100 true, false and cannot tell questions

This chapter contains 20 passages and 100 practice questions. You are bound to face these reading comprehension and critical reasoning questions at some stage in your career as they are fast becoming the most common type of verbal reasoning test question.

Each passage is following by five questions. Your task is to answer the questions by referring to each passage. You must determine if the correct answer is true, false or that you cannot tell (ie, you cannot tell if the answer is true or false). The questions require you, for example, to comprehend meaning and significance, assess logical strength, identify valid inference, distinguish between a main idea and a subordinate one, recognize the writer's intention and identify a valid summary, interpretation, or conclusion.

The subject of the passage can be drawn from a great many fields including current affairs, business, science, the environment, economics, history, metrology, health or education. If you know something of the subject then take care not to bring your own knowledge to the passage; you are expected to answer the questions using only the information it contains. Be especially careful if you know a great deal on the subject or if you believe the passage to be factually incorrect or controversial. It is not a test of your general knowledge or your personal opinions, so feel completely at ease about answering true to a statement which is true in the very limited context of the passage.

When a publisher of real tests develops a verbal reasoning test they rely on fine distinctions between the suggested answers in order to distinguish between the scores of the large numbers of candidates. These distinctions are much finer than we draw on a day-to-day basis. As a result it is common for candidates to feel irritation and complain that these tests are to a large extent arbitrary. In a way they are, after all this is not how we use language at work or anywhere else except in the surreal world of tests. This is something you just have to accept and get used to, and with practice you will get to recognize the subtle distinctions being drawn.

Take care not to err too much towards the 'cannot tell' suggested answer by making the mistake of applying too strict or too inflexible a test of proof. Be sure to read the questions as carefully as you read the passage and learn to pick up the many clues provided in the wording. The only way to master these subtle differences is to practise. You will soon gain more confidence and get better at making the proper judgements.

If when taking lots of time in the relaxed conditions of your home you find these questions easy, take care that you do not slip into a false sense of security. In a real test you will be pressed for time and may well be suffering from some anxiety. You should aim at carefully reading the passage once and then refer back to it in order to answer the question. Some people find it helps to read the questions before the passage.

You will find more practice questions of this type in the following Kogan Page titles: at the intermediate level, *The Ultimate Psychometric Test Book;* and at the advanced level, *The Graduate Psychometric Workbook, How to Pass Graduate Psychometric Tests,* 3rd edition and *How To Pass Advanced Verbal Reasoning Tests.*

Passage 1

Sour tasting things contain acids. They are only weak solutions of acid as something that is strongly acidic will burn human skin. A bee sting contains an acid, our stomach contains hydrochloric acid and a car battery contains a very strong solution of sulphuric acid. Acids are very widely used in the chemical industry. Pollution from power stations causes acid rain, which kills trees and fish.

1. It can be inferred from the passage that the hydrochloric acid in our stomachs is weak.

    True
    False
    Cannot tell   **Answer**   T

2. The primary purpose of the passage is to describe the properties of things that taste sour.

    True
    False
    Cannot tell   **Answer**   F

3. It can be inferred from the passage that the acid in a car battery would burn if it made contact with our skin.

    True
    False
    Cannot tell   **Answer**   C

4. A wasp sting contains an acid.

    True
    False
    Cannot tell   **Answer**   C

5. Lemon juice is an example of a sour tasting thing that is mentioned in the passage.

   True
   False
   Cannot tell **Answer** C

Passage 2

The ancient Greek Olympics were held at Olympia near the shore of the Ionian Sea for 1,000 years. These games were named after the snow peaked mount Olympus situated hundreds of miles away to the east near the Aegean Sea where it was thought the gods and goddesses lived, looking down on mankind. The ancient site of Olympia was excavated in the 19th century and the finds inspired the founding of the modern Olympics held every four years since the first modern games in 1896. The ancient games were intended to determine what metal – gold, silver or bronze – the athlete's heart was made of. In the modern Olympics medals of gold, silver and bronze are awarded to the athletes. The modern games also commemorate an ancient battle at Marathon where a Greek army defeated a much larger Persian force.

6. Both the excavation of Olympia and the first modern games occurred in the 19th century.

   True
   False
   Cannot tell **Answer** T

7. It can be determined from the passage that the Aegean Sea is east of the Ionian Sea.

   True
   False
   Cannot tell **Answer**

8. The ancient Greeks thought that the gods and goddesses lived in Olympia.

   True
   False
   Cannot tell   **Answer**   F

9. In the modern Olympics the athlete in first place receives a gold medal, silver is awarded for second place and bronze for third place.

   True
   False
   Cannot tell   **Answer**   T

10. In the context of the passage the word Marathon refers to a long-distance run.

   True
   False
   Cannot tell   **Answer**   F

Passage 3

It has always been known that bright children from high income households perform better academically than bright children from low income households. This inequality places the bright child from a low income household at a considerable disadvantage and this has repercussions for the rest of their lives. A bright child from a high income household is very likely to go to one of the country's top universities and is also very likely to enjoy a high income during their working lives. A bright child from a low income household is far less likely to win a place at any university let alone the country's top colleges. They are also likely to earn no more than the national average wage during their working lives.

11. The main theme in the passage is the advantages enjoyed by bright children from high income households.

    True
    False
    Cannot tell

    Answer [T]

12. In the context of the passage, high income household means one in which the combined income is in excess of $50,000 per annum.

    True
    False
    Cannot tell

    Answer [CT]

13. The fact that bright children from low income households do less well than bright children from high income families is not something that has only just been realized.

    True
    False
    Cannot tell

    Answer [T]

14. The author of the passage is likely to agree with the statement that a very bright child from a low income household is very likely to go to university.

    True
    False
    Cannot tell

    Answer [F]

15. If true, the fact that some bright children from low income house-holds do gain places at university would weaken the claim in the passage that bright children from low income households are far less likely to win a place at any university than bright children from high income households.

True

False

Cannot tell   **Answer**

Passage 4

They are unable to fly in the true sense but the many species of penguin are all very adept swimmers. They literally 'fly' underwater using their wings as flippers and their feet and tails to steer as they hunt fish and squid, which form the bulk of their diet. This extraordinary family of birds feed in the cold waters of the southern oceans (they are only found in the wild in the southern hemisphere). Their bodies are highly adapted both for their aquatic life and for the cold. Their feathers are short and dense to provide insulation and a highly waterproof layer. Their bones are not hollow like most birds but solid, making them stronger and less buoyant, helping them dive deep down to their prey. Like all birds they lay eggs and most species build nests, but some that live on sheet ice in the Antarctic, where there is no nest-building material, incubate their single egg on the top of their feet.

16. In the passage, solid bones are described as an adaptation for the cold southern climate.

True

False

Cannot tell   **Answer**

17. It can be inferred from the passage that you have to go to the southern hemisphere if you wish to see penguins in the wild.

    True
    False
    Cannot tell   **Answer** [T]

18. Penguins are not unique in being flightless birds.

    True
    False
    Cannot tell   **Answer** [CT]

19. The passage states that penguins lay a single egg.

    True
    False
    Cannot tell   **Answer** [CT]

20. The sentiment of the passage can be captured by the statement that penguins are an extraordinary family of birds.

    True
    False
    Cannot tell   **Answer** [T]

Passage 5

The first time a single German nation existed was in 1871 when Wilhelm the 1st became Emperor and Bismarck Chancellor. The unified Germany became a great economic and military power, and empire, but defeat in the two World Wars led to its break-up in 1945 into East and West Germany. At that time the Berlin Wall was built and served to separate East from West. In 1990 the wall was demolished and Germany was unified once again.

21. Germany has been unified as a nation on three occasions.

    True
    False
    Cannot tell   **Answer**   T

22. The passage suggests two reasons for the break-up of Germany in 1945.

    True
    False
    Cannot tell   **Answer**   F

23. The author may well agree with the statement that a reunified Germany will once again become a great economic and military power.

    True
    False
    Cannot tell   **Answer**   CT

24. The Berlin Wall is mentioned in the passage in relation to the countries' reunification in 1990.

    True
    False
    Cannot tell   **Answer**   T

25. You can correctly infer from the passage that the Berlin Wall stood for 45 years.

    True
    False
    Cannot tell   **Answer**   T

Passage 6

The era of mass media is giving way to one of personal and participatory media. Technology has freed people from having to passively consume mass media content. They are beginning to value their own opinions and offer them online alongside those of the supposed experts. They post online ratings for their favourite restaurant, and they contribute entries to collaborative sites offering advice and answers to questions posed on every imaginable subject. They are quickly realizing that all too often the views of a rank amateur are as or even more interesting than those of the experts. It is only the beginning of a revolution that will encircle the globe and affect most people as access to the internet becomes even more widespread.

26. The passage presents what can be described as a counter argument or at least an alternative perspective.

    True
    False
    Cannot tell   **Answer**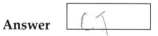

27. When the passage was written there was no universal access to the internet.

    True
    False
    Cannot tell   **Answer**

28. The penultimate sentence of the passage illustrates the sort of things that people post online.

    True
    False
    Cannot tell   **Answer**

29. The subject of how the large traditional media corporations will respond to the challenge of the internet is touched upon in the passage.

True
False
Cannot tell   **Answer**   T

30. Not everything posted on the internet is correct and sometimes people's contributions are misleading.

True
False
Cannot tell   **Answer**   CT

Passage 7

Paperback books were made popular by the publisher Penguin in the 1930s. They are less expensive to manufacture than hardback books, so they can be sold at a lower price and achieve far higher unit sales. Producing a book, whether paper or hardback, involves a good many people and can easily take two years from conception to publication. The author begins the process, researching and writing a proposal for the title. A publishing committee discusses the commercial viability of the idea and takes the decision on whether or not to invest in the title and publish it. The author then writes a manuscript which nowadays is submitted in a digital form. Editors and designers work on the manuscript and produce what is called the proof, which is sent to the printer to be typeset and printed. A team of sales representatives visit book stores and online bookshop buyers and promote the title. Copy-writers list and promote the book. Finally, distributors deliver copies of the book to bookstores and directly to customers.

31. The principal subject of the passage is a description of the process of producing paperback books.

    True
    False
    Cannot tell   **Answer**   F

32. A justification for the lower price of paperback books is offered in the passage.

    True
    False
    Cannot tell   **Answer**   T

33. The passage assumes no prior knowledge of the publishing industry.

    True
    False
    Cannot tell   **Answer**   T

34. Penguin is still a major publisher of paperback books.

    True
    False
    Cannot tell   **Answer**   T

35. The author is responsible for the production of the proof.

    True
    False
    Cannot tell   **Answer**   F

Passage 8

From outer space the world looks blue because of the extent that oceans cover its surface and of all the oceans the greatest is the Pacific. It stretches from the Arctic to the Antarctic, more than halfway around the globe and is twice the size of the next biggest ocean, the Atlantic. It harbours trenches 11,000m deep, which makes it the deepest of the oceans. Along its rim are some of the world's richest nations. Huge cargo ships cross it carrying minerals, such as iron ore and copper from Australia, and manufactured goods from Japan, China and the United States. More than half the world's catch of fish is from the Pacific. Most of the world's palm oil is manufactured from the dried flesh of coconuts on the over 20,000 islands of the Pacific.

36. It can be inferred from the passage that there are five oceans of which the Pacific is the largest.

    True
    False
    Cannot tell   **Answer** [F]

37. The Pacific accounts for more than half of the globe's surface area taken up by ocean.

    True
    False
    Cannot tell   **Answer** [F]

38. It can be concluded that no other ocean contains a trench 11,000m deep.

    True
    False
    Cannot tell   **Answer** [T]

39. It is possible to travel by ship from the Arctic to the Antarctic without leaving the Pacific ocean.

    True
    False
    Cannot tell **Answer**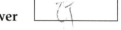

40. The sentiment of the passage is captured by the statement 'of all the oceans the greatest is the Pacific'.

    True
    False
    Cannot tell **Answer**

Passage 9

We like to think of ourselves as unique but we are in fact 99.9 per cent genetically identical. DNA, which comprises the chemical code, governs the construction and function of every cell in our body. The Human Genome Project mapped the sequence for human DNA and provided a blueprint of the DNA shared by every person. But what of the 0.1 per cent that is not common to all mankind and was left out of the Human Genome Project blueprint? It is responsible for all individual idiosyncrasies and the differences between racial and ethnic groups. If it were not for this minute percentage there would be no individual differences. We would be clones. Individual differences could be greatly increased if we were to think the unthinkable and allow genetic engineering of the human DNA. This would involve inserting genes from one cell into another and changing that cell's DNA and its characteristics. In theory it would be possible to take the DNA from an entirely different species and insert it into human cells. Such radical modifications could certainly make us much more unique.

41. In the context of the passage idiosyncrasies means unconventional behaviour.

   True
   False
   Cannot tell   **Answer**   [T]

42. It can be inferred from the passage that the author does not approve of the genetic engineering of human DNA.

   True
   False
   Cannot tell   **Answer**   [C T]

43. The Human Genome Project is mentioned in the project in relation to cloning.

   True
   False
   Cannot tell   **Answer**   [F]

44. A word that means the same as blueprint is design.

   True
   False
   Cannot tell   **Answer**   [T]

45. It can be inferred from the passage that a DNA molecule is contained in the nucleus of every cell in our body.

   True
   False
   Cannot tell   **Answer**   [F]

Passage 10

Many young people drift into university because they do not know what else to do. They leave years later, often in considerable debt, and find that a degree is no longer a guaranteed route into a good job. In fact the number of graduates is increasing at a much faster rate than the number of graduate jobs. They also find that there are plenty of careers that do not need a university degree and for these jobs they must compete with the many non-graduate job seekers. In law enforcement, public administration, nursing, catering, retail, construction and transport there are many highly paid roles wide open to the non-graduate. Take for example an airline pilot. No degree is required for this post and salaries routinely start at $100,000. Another example is the manager of a supermarket. No degree is needed yet they are responsible for the running of a business that grosses millions of dollars a month and employs hundreds of people. Managers of the larger stores are on salaries far in excess of $100,000.

46. The case made in the passage would be weakened if it were true that the large majority of graduates find good jobs on leaving university.

    True
    False
    Cannot tell   **Answer**

47. The author of the passage is of the view that the role of airline pilot is highly paid.

    True
    False
    Cannot tell   **Answer**

48. We cannot infer from the passage that it was once the case that a degree was considered a guaranteed route into a good job.

    True
    False
    Cannot tell   **Answer** [T   ]

49. The passage gives a positive reason for why many people go to university.

    True
    False
    Cannot tell   **Answer** [Ø   T]

50. The passage touches on the reason why a degree is not a route into a good job.

    True
    False
    Cannot tell   **Answer** [   ]

Passage 11

A solid is any piece of matter that has a definite shape and volume. A liquid has no fixed shape but does have a definite volume. This means that you can drop a solid and, depending on how 'solid' it is, it will keep its shape. If it is highly plastic then it may lose its original shape and be reshaped into another one by the force of the fall. If it is highly elastic it may lose its shape momentarily but then regain it. If it is very brittle it may break into a great many pieces – none are lost but it has taken on a new, fragmented shape. A solid with great strength is unlikely to be affected by being dropped. Pour a liquid and it will spread out into an irregular shape. A liquid that has a high viscosity will spread out far more slowly than a liquid with a low viscosity. When we pour a liquid none of it is lost (the volume is the same), it has simply taken a different shape. If we heat a solid it may well turn into a liquid.

51. According to the passage both solids and liquids have definite volumes.

     True
     False
     Cannot tell   **Answer** [T]

52. If we cool a liquid it will turn into a solid.

     True
     False
     Cannot tell   **Answer** [CT]

53. In the context of the passage the word matter means substance.

     True
     False
     Cannot tell   **Answer** [T]

54. Two reasons are given as to why a solid may lose its shape if dropped.

     True
     False
     Cannot tell   **Answer** [F]

55. A description of the qualities of a solid if dropped is a subsidiary theme
     of the passage.

     True
     False
     Cannot tell   **Answer** [T]

Passage 12

The vast majority of citizens believe that the official statistics produced by governments are subject to political interference. They accuse opposition parties and pressure groups of the same interference and all three of using figures in wildly misleading ways to support their particular take on policy. The only difference is that governments are accused of using the figures to make the best possible case, opposition parties of taking the least favourable interpretation and pressure groups of selecting only the figures that prove their case. The media are considered just as guilty. Bad news is much more newsworthy than good news and people complain that we hear little other than a stream of stories suggesting that life is awful and getting worse. No wonder public trust in official data is at an all time low.

56. You cannot tell from the passage if the author agrees with the vast majority of citizens.

    True
    False
    Cannot tell   **Answer** | ~~F~~ T |

57. In the passage, governments in particular are subjected to criticism.

    True
    False
    Cannot tell   **Answer** | T |

58. The term 'all time low' means that public trust in official data has never been lower but may have been as low before.

    True
    False
    Cannot tell   **Answer** | F |

59. It can be inferred from the passage that good news is not newsworthy.

   True
   False
   Cannot tell   **Answer** F

60. Public trust in governments, opposition parties, pressure groups and the media is at an all time low.

   True
   False
   Cannot tell   **Answer** CT

Passage 13

NASA, the US space agency, announced plans to return to the moon in 15 years and the plan is to stay. It was 1972 when the last people stepped on the moon. The next time an astronaut walks there he or she is most likely to visit the polar region rather than the equatorial zone, the site of all previous missions. The poles are the preferred location because they experience more moderate temperatures and are bathed in almost continuous sunlight which will allow a permanent research station to be powered by solar power. Another benefit of the polar regions is that they are believed to hold mineral deposits from which oxygen and hydrogen can be extracted. And with oxygen and hydrogen the astronauts will be able to make water. After a number of robotic scouting missions a great many short duration manned transportation missions would take place. These missions would deliver the components necessary to build the moon station.

61. We can expect the next moon mission to take place in 15 years time.

   True
   False
   Cannot tell   **Answer**

62. The question of where the astronauts will get their water from is answered in the passage.

    True
    False
    Cannot tell

    Answer

63. The following are all referred to in the passage: mineral deposits, the moon base's power source, the landing site for the next moon mission and the date of the last manned moon mission.

    True
    False
    Cannot tell

    Answer

64. The last manned mission to the moon in 1972 included a women astronaut.

    True
    False
    Cannot tell

    Answer C T

65. The tone of the passage is fatalistic.

    True
    False
    Cannot tell

    Answer F

Passage 14

Mention Australia and people think of sunshine, beaches and coral reefs. Mention the interior of Australia and people only think of the arid outback and desert. But Australia also has extensive rain forests, mountain ranges (a few with snow) and wetlands. It has rivers too, the mightiest of which is the Murray. It stretches over 2,500 km from its source high in the interior mountains to its mouth. Much of its length forms the boundary between the Australian states Victoria and New South Wales and it was once a busy waterway used to carry wheat, wool and timber from the interior to the city of Melbourne. Nowadays the river is quiet, not because the farming and lumbering has stopped but because the produce is carried by train and truck instead.

66. The word arid means dry.

    True
    False
    Cannot tell   **Answer** [   ]

67. It can be inferred from the passage that Australia's interior has more diverse habitats than people think.

    True
    False
    Cannot tell   **Answer** [   ]

68. You can still navigate the river Murray in a boat but the work of transporting produce has been lost to trains and trucks.

    True
    False
    Cannot tell   **Answer** [   ]

69. The author is unlikely to agree with the view that the beaches and coral reefs are less interesting than the interior of Australia.

True
False
Cannot tell   **Answer**

70. The tone of the passage is sceptical.

True
False
Cannot tell   **Answer**

Passage 15

Road signs and traffic lights at junctions and busy crossing points may be removed in order to improve road safety. The suggestion to remove road signs to improve road safety seems contradictory and certainly goes against the fashion of separating and controlling traffic and pedestrians. The idea is to create anxiety, principally in the mind of drivers, so that they slow down and pay greater attention. Current demarcations between pavement and road will be made indistinct by removing railings and kerbs, resurfacing both in the same material and re-laying them so that they are on the same level. Neither the driver nor pedestrian will then feel they have right of way and as a consequence both will behave more cautiously.

71. If the volume of traffic were to increase by 50 per cent the case made in the passage would be weakened.

True
False
Cannot tell   **Answer**

72. The views expressed in the passage are a statement of the findings of experimental investigations.

    True
    False
    Cannot tell   **Answer**

73. We can infer from the passage that the proposed removal of road signs and traffic lights is to go ahead.

    True
    False
    Cannot tell   **Answer**

74. The word 'principally' in the passage means only.

    True
    False
    Cannot tell   **Answer**

75. The author is cynical of the proposal to remove road signs and traffic lights.

    True
    False
    Cannot tell   **Answer**

Passage 16

The City of Manchester in England was at the forefront of the 19th century industrial revolution and a global centre for the manufacture of cotton cloth. The city's industry is no longer centred on manufacturing but on service-based commerce, in particular finance and insurance. Manchester's architecture reflects this change and is a mix of buildings that date back to the times of the cotton trade and more contemporary constructions including the Beetham Tower, the tallest building outside of London, and The Green Building, a pioneering eco-friendly housing project. Most of the many ex-cotton mills still exist but have been converted into luxury apartments, hotels and office space. It is estimated that 35 per cent of Manchester's population has Irish ancestry and the Manchester Irish Festival and St Patrick's Day Parade are among the most popular of the many events that take place in the city.

76. You can infer from the passage that cotton is grown in the vicinity of Manchester.

    True
    False
    Cannot tell   **Answer**

77. The passage was probably written in the 21st century.

    True
    False
    Cannot tell   **Answer**

78. The subject of the passage is the architecture of the city of Manchester.

    True
    False
    Cannot tell   **Answer**

79. You can infer from the author saying, 'The City of Manchester in England' that there are other cities in the world called Manchester and the author wanted to identify which of them he was referring to.

    True
    False
    Cannot tell   **Answer**

80. The tone of the passage is buoyant.

    True
    False
    Cannot tell   **Answer**

Passage 17

Intellectual property infers the right to extort payment when our cultural expression should be free and freely shared. In the digital world everyone is an author, publisher and critic so why should a chosen few be allowed to lay claim to the expression of our common cultural heritage and enjoy the recognition of authorship and the right to royalties? Why should the corporate media conglomerates be allowed to use copyright, patents and intellectual property laws to make criminals of tens of thousands of users of virtual communities if they share music, videos and written works? These users freely share their own work and if all work were to be donated in this way the public sphere would be a far more cultural, creative place.

81. The word conglomerate means large business.

    True
    False
    Cannot tell   **Answer**

82. The author would agree that a musician should receive payment when his work is broadcast.

    True
    False
    Cannot tell   **Answer** [   ]

83. The author would agree that I should be able to walk into a bookshop and take any of the works found there without paying.

    True
    False
    Cannot tell   **Answer** [   ]

84. The sentiment of the passage is captured in the statement 'the public sphere would be a far more cultural, creative place'.

    True
    False
    Cannot tell   **Answer** [   ]

85. In the passage the statement 'Why should the corporate media conglomerates be allowed to use copyright, patents and intellectual property laws to make criminals of tens of thousands of users of virtual communities if they share music, videos and written works?' is relied upon as a premise to the conclusion that 'if all work were to be donated in this way the public sphere would be a far more cultural, creative place.'

    True
    False
    Cannot tell   **Answer** [   ]

Passage 18

Diamonds are transparent and graphite is dark grey – both are forms of the element carbon, a non metal. Diamonds are the hardest naturally occurring material. Graphite is a very good conductor of electricity. Both are crystalline in form. There are a great number of carbon-based compounds and many are found in living tissue. Fossilized plants can form an impure form of carbon called coal. If we heat wood in the absence of air we make another impure form of carbon called charcoal. Carbon fibres are used to manufacture things that need to be strong but light.

86. The passage states that the element carbon has two naturally occurring pure forms, diamonds and graphite.

    True
    False
    Cannot tell   **Answer**

87. The passage described three qualities of diamonds.

    True
    False
    Cannot tell   **Answer**

88. It can be inferred from the passage that all living tissues are made up of carbon-based compounds.

    True
    False
    Cannot tell   **Answer**

89. The subject of the passage is the element carbon.

   True
   False
   Cannot tell   **Answer** ⎸_____⎹

90. The author would agree that we use carbon fibre to manufacture things that need to be strong but light because it is stronger than other materials of the same weight.

   True
   False
   Cannot tell   **Answer** ⎸_____⎹

Passage 19

In northern communities it is not just shift workers and people who fly long distances who find their daily life out of phase with the natural wake-sleep/light-dark cycle. In winter in those high latitudes most workers rise hours before sun-rise. In the summer months they rely on heavy curtains to darken a room from the evening sun so that they can sleep. It is not just the wake-sleep rhythm that is affected: blood pressure, body temperature, reaction times, appetite and levels of alertness all follow a daily cycle and are synchronized with light and dark. Doctors recognize that a mismatch between the many demands of modern life and the hours of light and darkness leads to increases in many disorders. Weight gain, gastrointestinal complaints and depression are the most common.

91. People's mental heath is stated as something that may be affected if their daily life is out of phase with the natural wake-sleep/light-dark cycle.

   True
   False
   Cannot tell   **Answer** ⎸_____⎹

92. The author would agree that only people who live in high latitudes find their busy lives out of phase with the natural wake-sleep/light-dark cycle.

    True
    False
    Cannot tell   **Answer** [   ]

93. In the context of the passage latitude means being allowed the freedom to lead a life that might adversely affect your health.

    True
    False
    Cannot tell   **Answer** [   ]

94. The passage compares the problems people who work shifts and fly long distances face with those of people living in northern communities.

    True
    False
    Cannot tell   **Answer** [   ]

95. In winter in northern communities school children must also get up before it is light.

    True
    False
    Cannot tell   **Answer** [   ]

Passage 20

Many people wonder why children aren't taught grammar and punctuation at school. Many of our teachers today are the product of the same education system that they now teach in and so the simple answer is that they have never learnt it themselves. In recent years there have been significant improvements in the level of functional literacy amongst school leavers, but at the other end of the range universities are complaining about the poor writing skills of undergraduates. These complaints are not raised because of a failure by students to place an adverb in the correct place or to leave out the prepositional phrase. They are far more fundamental failures, such as incorrect use of apostrophes and confused tenses.

96. The meaning of the sentence would be unaffected if we substituted the words significant and range with meaningful and spectrum.

    True
    False
    Cannot tell   **Answer**

97. The passage says that teachers can't teach grammar and punctuation because they have not been taught it themselves.

    True
    False
    Cannot tell   **Answer**

98. The teaching of grammar and punctuation does not feature in the school curriculum.

    True
    False
    Cannot tell   **Answer**

99. The author would agree that the reading and writing skills of children of school leaving age have improved.

True
False
Cannot tell   **Answer** [   ]

100. The author does not think that placing an adverb in the wrong place or leaving out a prepositional phrase are elementary errors in grammar.

True
False
Cannot tell   **Answer** [   ]

6

Four full-length realistic practice tests

This chapter provides four practice tests. Use them to develop a good exam technique and improve your stamina and endurance under test conditions.

In each test the time allowed, number and level of difficulty of the questions and the competencies tested are similar to real intermediate verbal reasoning tests used by employers. Undertake them in conditions that are as realistic as possible. Find yourself a quiet place where you will be able to work for the suggested time limit without interruption. Approach each test as if it were the real thing and apply the sheer hard work and continuous concentration essential to a good score in a real test. Practise effective management of your time and remember not to spend too long on any one question.

To create a truly realistic test experience, set yourself the personal challenge of trying to beat your last score each time you take one of these practice tests (when you score each test, allow yourself one mark per question). You will need to try really hard and take the challenge seriously if you are to realize this aim.

After each test review your answers and go over the explanations for those you got wrong. You should aim to understand the gaps in your knowledge. Before you take the next test, set about further practice of the sort found in earlier chapters with the intention of reviewing the principles you do not fully understand. Use the interpretation of your score to determine the amount and type of practice you still need.

Practice test 1: Verbal reasoning

In this test you are given three words – a pair of words and a word with its pair missing. You must try to identify the relationship that exists between the complete pair before choosing a word from a list that has a similar relationship with the single word.

You are allowed 30 minutes in which to complete the 40 questions. Work quickly and without interruption and write the number or letter of the word of your choice in the answer box.

If you find a series of questions difficult, keep going as you may find that you reach questions later on for which you are better prepared. Remember that in order to do well in a test you have to try really hard.

Do not turn over the page until you are ready to begin.

1. Boat   Sails
    Car   ?

    A   Engine
    B   Tyres
    C   Journeys
    D   Motorbikes   **Answer**

2. Fire   Smoke
    Words   ?

    A   Letters
    B   Sentences
    C   Voices
    D   Dictionary   **Answer**

3. Telephone   ?
    River   Sea

    A   Receiver
    B   Ring tone
    C   Conversation
    D   Exchange   **Answer**

4. Surface   ?
    Fuzzy   Smooth

    A   Veneer
    B   Interior
    C   Appearance
    D   Horizontal   **Answer**

5. Jailed   Fraud
   Expelled   ?

       A   School
       B   Smoking
       C   Kick off
       D   Child   **Answer**

6. ?   Engineer
   Swan   Bird

       A   Mechanical
       B   Scientist
       C   Project
       D   Professional   **Answer**

7. ?   Mushy
   Polish   Waxy

       A   Feeble
       B   Soup
       C   Baby food
       D   Sentimental   **Answer**

8. Height   Weight
   Joyous   ?

       A   Beautiful
       B   Attractive
       C   Sombre
       D   Occasion   **Answer**

9. Inflate   ?
   Guess   Estimate

   A   Magnify
   B   Deflate
   C   Solve
   D   Expand   **Answer** ☐

10. Sensible   Stupid
    Opaque   ?

    A   Cloudy
    B   Transparent
    C   Obscure
    D   Dumb   **Answer** ☐

11. Pages   Book
    ?   Cloth

    A   Yarns
    B   Cloths
    C   Fibres
    D   Yard   **Answer** ☐

12. ?   Key
    Violin   Bow

    A   Ship
    B   Arrow
    C   Musical note
    D   Lock   **Answer** ☐

13. Barley   Cereal
    Parliament   ?

    A   Election
    B   Democracy
    C   Assembly
    D   Government   **Answer**

14. Photosynthesis   Sunlight
    ?   Concert

    A   Hall
    B   Symphony
    C   Orchestra
    D   Performance   **Answer**

15. Acid   Alkali
    Lax   ?

    A   Slack
    B   Blame
    C   Strict
    D   Casual   **Answer**

16. Microscope   ?
    Language   Communication

    A   Exploration
    B   Magnification
    C   Population
    D   Classification   **Answer**

17. ?   Crate
Divide   Distribute

   A   Disturbance
   B   Vegetables
   C   Chaos
   D   Chest   **Answer**

18. Proponent   Supporter
?   Myth

   A   Hero
   B   Sorcerer
   C   Story
   D   Truth   **Answer**

19. Painkiller   ?
Hockey   Ballgame

   A   Medicine
   B   Cure
   C   Compound
   D   Sport   **Answer**

20. Natural   ?
Convict   Acquit

   A   Wholesome
   B   Spoiled
   C   Virtuous
   D   Synthetic   **Answer**

21. Geology   Science
    Statistics   ?

    A   Knowledge
    B   Mathematics
    C   Probability
    D   Business Studies   **Answer**

22. Oblong   ?
    Set square   Ruler

    A   Circumference
    B   Chart
    C   Cuboid
    D   Hoop   **Answer**

23. ?   Weaken
    Refuse   Decline

    A   Dilute
    B   Destroy
    C   Poorly
    D   Brittle   **Answer**

24. Construction   Transport
    Turtle   ?

    A   Dove
    B   Bird
    C   Animal
    D   Lizard   **Answer**

25. Flyover   Viaduct
    ?   Ayatollah

    A   Archbishop
    B   Islam
    C   Religion
    D   Prayers   **Answer**

26. Tabloid   Broadsheet
    ?   Spanish

    1   European
    2   Hindi
    3   Mediterranean
    4   Asia   **Answer**

27. ?   Surf
    Candle   Light

    1   Washing powder
    2   Sport
    3   Ripple
    4   Waves   **Answer**

28. Graphite   ?
    Furniture   Wood

    1   Pencil
    2   Slippery
    3   Organic
    4   Carbon   **Answer**

29. Medicine   Cure
       ?   Warmth

   1   Summer
   2   Insulation
   3   Hospitality
   4   Fire   **Answer**

30. House   Bricks
     Pension   ?

   1   Financial institution
   2   Savings
   3   Retirement
   4   Contributions   **Answer**

31. Inference   ?
     Seed   Plant

   1   Premise
   2   Slander
   3   Conclusion
   4   Reaction   **Answer**

32. Cruel   ?
     Harmony   Discord

   1   Inhumane
   2   Sadistic
   3   Criminal
   4   Humane   **Answer**

33. Air   Breathe
    ?   Solution

    1   Problem
    2   Answer
    3   Liquid
    4   Compound   **Answer**

34. ?   Ascend
    Pledge   Guarantee

    1   Block
    2   Scale
    3   Descend
    4   Retract   **Answer**

35. Pencil   Art
    ?   Telecommunications

    1   Phone
    2   Communication
    3   Watch dog
    4   Artist   **Answer**

36. Sun   ?
    Criticism   Anger

    1   Day
    2   Tan
    3   Burn
    4   Light   **Answer**

37. Know   No
    ?   Site

    1   Sight
    2   Location
    3   Situation
    4   Building   **Answer**

38. Music   Pleasure
    ?   Discovery

    1   Loss
    2   Research
    3   Find
    4   Adventure   **Answer**

39. Outspoken   Reserved
    General   ?

    1   Specific
    2   Generic
    3   Officer
    4   Widespread   **Answer**

40. Mushroom   Plunge
    ?   Late

    1   Night
    2   Hamper
    3   Invitation
    4   Punctual   **Answer**

End of test.

Practice test 2: Verbal reasoning

This style of question requires you to identify a word or phrase that means the same or the opposite or is closest in meaning. The practice you have undertaken in Chapters 2 and 3 will have prepared you well for this test, so to make it more of a challenge I have added a twist. Read this carefully. In this test you are presented with a single word or phrase and below it a list numbered 1–4 from which you must identify the answer. You must first decide if the question word and the word numbered 1 in the list are synonyms or antonyms. If they are the answer is 1. If they are not then you must look to the rest of the list to identify a synonym or antonym **of either the question word or the word numbered 1 in the list** (and record the corresponding number 2, 3 or 4 in the answer box).

With practice you can greatly improve your performance in this sort of test. If you find these questions difficult, set about expanding your vocabulary and confidence by reading a quality newspaper every day and looking up words whose meaning you do not know in a dictionary or thesaurus. A thesaurus (which lists words of similar meaning) is really helpful in better understanding the answers to these questions.

You are allowed 25 minutes in which to complete the 35 questions. Work quickly and without interruption.

If you find a series of questions difficult, keep going; you may find that you reach questions later on for which you are better prepared. Remember that to do well in a test you have to try really hard.

Do not turn over the page until you are ready to begin.

1. Head-on   ?

    1   Hurried
    2   Head off
    3   Head for
    4   Headlong   **Answer**

2. Prevention   ?

    1   Cure
    2   Avoidance
    3   Evasion
    4   Safety   **Answer**

3. Decisive   ?

    1   Deceptive
    2   Tortuous
    3   Truthful
    4   Decision   **Answer**

4. Investigate   ?

    1   Detective
    2   Ignorant
    3   Ignore
    4   Inquest   **Answer**

5. Salute   ?

    1   Acknowledge
    2   Plaudit
    3   Obey
    4   Slight   **Answer**

6. Unorthodox   ?

    1   Probable
    2   Credible
    3   Topic
    4   Protect   **Answer**

7. Assessment   ?

    1   Evaluation
    2   Incident
    3   Strong point
    4   Situation   **Answer**

8. Relationship   ?

    1   Habitually
    2   Lesson
    3   Far-reaching
    4   Seldom   **Answer**

9. Escape   ?

    1   Lucky
    2   Route
    3   Remain
    4   Plan   **Answer**

10. Glaring   ?

    1   Dazzling
    2   Rich
    3   Explode
    4   Discharge   **Answer**

11. Regulations   ?

    1   Safety
    2   Chaos
    3   Anarchy
    4   Code   **Answer**

12. Nurture   ?

    1   Accomplish
    2   Venerate
    3   Attain
    4   Exclaim   **Answer**

13. Affirmative   ?

    1   Swear
    2   Comfort
    3   Declare
    4   Negative   **Answer**

14. Idea   ?

    1   Thorough
    2   Kind
    3   Methodical
    4   Inconsiderate   **Answer**

15. Support   ?

    1   Install
    2   Brace
    3   Go backwards
    4   Return   **Answer**

16. Open   ?

    1   Unused
    2   Pristine
    3   Fake
    4   Firsthand   **Answer**

17. Ignore   ?

    1   Insult
    2   Forget
    3   Consult
    4   Lose   **Answer**

18. Onlooker   ?

    1   Bystander
    2   Security
    3   Accomplice
    4   Shopper   **Answer**

19. Comfort   ?

    1   Solemn
    2   Informal
    3   Blunder
    4   Solitary   **Answer**

20. Utilize   ?

    1   Organize
    2   Use up
    3   Knife and fork
    4   Deploy   **Answer**

21. Fiscal   ?

   1 Economical
   2 Generous
   3 Business
   4 Careful   **Answer**

22. Neighbourly   ?

   1 Sociable
   2 Collective
   3 Public
   4 Team player   **Answer**

23. Launch   ?

   1 Terminate
   2 Ultimate
   3 Incurable
   4 Inherit   **Answer**

24. Drought   ?

   1 Drunk
   2 Deluge
   3 Drown
   4 Famine   **Answer**

25. Tangible   ?

   1 Untangle
   2 Intricate
   3 Painstaking
   4 Entangle   **Answer**

26. Enslave   ?

    1   Criminal
    2   Colonial
    3   Liberate
    4   Genocide   **Answer** ☐

27. Harm   ?

    1   Restrain
    2   Injure
    3   Cover
    4   Dry   **Answer** ☐

28. Forthright   ?

    1   Debate
    2   Conceal
    3   Forth place
    4   Wrong   **Answer** ☐

29. Resistant   ?

    1   Incombustible
    2   Protectable
    3   Flameproof
    4   Safe   **Answer** ☐

30. Affliction   ?

    1   Console
    2   Make worse
    3   Persecute
    4   Ordeal   **Answer** ☐

31. Speedy   ?

    1   Composure
    2   Moderate
    3   Panic
    4   Attractive   **Answer**

32. Collapse   ?

    1   Overthrow
    2   Disintegrate
    3   Defend
    4   Enflame   **Answer**

33. Interrupt   ?

    1   Continue
    2   Conditional
    3   Contention
    4   Contentious   **Answer**

34. Extinguish   ?

    1   Quench
    2   Squeeze
    3   Prevent
    4   Famous   **Answer**

35. Exile   ?

    1   Refuge
    2   Fugitive
    3   Decline
    4   Protection   **Answer**

End of test.

Practice test 3: Verbal usage

This test comprises 35 questions. You are allowed 25 minutes in which to attempt them. Each question consists of a sentence with words missing, then four combinations of words labelled A–D. You are required to identify the combination that is correct in terms of English usage. The solution may be a question of grammar, punctuation, spelling or style. Write the corresponding letter of the alphabet for the answer of your choice in the answer box.

Work somewhere free of interruption and complete the test in one continuous period.

Do not turn the page until you are ready to begin.

1. I've ___ for the train for some time but it seems ___ a few minutes ago.

   A   wait and its leaving
   B   waited and it leave
   C   wait and it's left
   D   been waiting and it left   **Answer**

2. I ___ had time to speak to him yet but I certainly will ___.

   A   haven't and tomorrow
   B   didn't and later today
   C   hadn't and tomorrow
   D   did not and later today   **Answer**

3. I read that a Peter Brown has just got the job of ___ engineer; do you think it is ___ Peter Brown we knew at university?

   A   a and a
   B   the and [no word needed]
   C   an and an
   D   [no word needed] and the   **Answer**

4. It was ___ outside but Joe still wanted an ___.

   A   ice cold and ice cream
   B   ice cold and ice-cream
   C   ice-cold and ice-cream
   D   ice-cold and icecream   **Answer**

5. It's not very likely but we ___ go to Egypt next year; however, we ___ go until after Christmas.

   A   may and shall
   B   might and shan't
   C   may and shan't
   D   might and shall   **Answer**

6. In the San Francisco earthquake of 1906 those few buildings ___ the earthquake ___ by the fire that followed.

   A   that survived and were destroyed
   B   that was destroyed in and was destroyed
   C   destroyed by and survived
   D   that survived and was destroyed   **Answer**

7. I want the job so ___ but they have told me I ___ stop smoking otherwise I can't have it.

   A   many and have to
   B   many and really must
   C   much and have got to
   D   much and am going to   **Answer**

8. The ___ doctor only treats ___.

   A   women and woman
   B   woman and women
   C   women and women
   D   woman and woman   **Answer**

9. They went ___ work by car and arrived ___ time.

   A   in and on
   B   to and on
   C   on and in
   D   at and at   **Answer**

10. I ___ a new friend at the library today.

   A   make
   B   meet
   C   met
   D   made   **Answer**

11. Until very recently there ___ an effective treatment for this serious disease.

    A   may not be
    B   used not to be
    C   there ought to be
    D   could not be   **Answer**

12. You ___ and cooked so much lovely food but it was lovely.

    A   didn't need to go
    B   needed to go
    C   needn't have gone
    D   needn't have go   **Answer**

13. They were beside themselves with anger ___ the news.

    A   at
    B   with
    C   for
    D   of   **Answer**

14. The price of crude oil is the highest ___ December 07, when a barrel passed the $100 mark.

    A   except
    B   but for
    C   but
    D   aside from   **Answer**

15. The boy agreed to care ___ the dog and walk it every day.

    A   about
    B   for
    C   with
    D   at   **Answer**

16. His son was born ___ noon ___ 5 January 2008.

    A   in and at
    B   at and in
    C   at and on
    D   on and at   **Answer**

17. ___ a really good bookshop on the high street but ___ is closed on Wednesdays.

    A   There is and it
    B   Theirs and it
    C   There's and there's
    D   It and its   **Answer**

18. The ___ I study the ___ I become.

    A   more hard and more intelligent
    B   harder and intelligenter
    C   more hard and more intelligenter
    D   harder and more intelligent   **Answer**

19. They went down to breakfast late to find that there weren't ___ eggs left only ___ bread rolls.

    A   any and any
    B   some and any
    C   some and some
    D   any and some   **Answer**

20. This is the artist ___ painted the picture ___ you really liked.

    A   whom and whom
    B   who and that
    C   that and which
    D   which and who   **Answer**

21. The bus seemed ___ ___

    A   such and big and red
    B   such and red and big
    C   so and big and red
    D   so and red and big   **Answer**

22. The boy had three sisters, two of ___ are older than him.

    A   which
    B   them
    C   they
    D   who   **Answer**

23. We had a fabulous day ___ the beach and returned home ___ bus.

    A   in and by
    B   at and in
    C   on and on
    D   at and by   **Answer**

24. He made his choice on the basis that the shoes were not ___ expensive as the Italian pair but ___ well made as the pair from Indonesia.

    A   so and as
    B   so and so
    C   as and as
    D   as and so   **Answer**

25. She rarely felt the need to ___ but on this occasion her friend suggested it would be for the ___.

    A   apology and better
    B   apologize and best
    C   apologize and much better
    D   apologies and much better   **Answer**

26. The ___ speech was found where he had left it ___ the plane.

    A   academic and at
    B   academic's and in
    C   academic's and on
    D   academic and with   **Answer**

27. I haven't ___ time but I will try to get to know as ___ of your friends as possible.

    A   much and much
    B   many and much
    C   much and many
    D   many and many   **Answer**

28. Although the train was ___ I still missed it because my watch was ___.

    A   early and late
    B   late and slow
    C   early and fast
    D   late and fast   **Answer**

29. ___ to eat in the restaurant for ages, so when my brother visited I invited him but he insisted ___ for the meal.

    A   I want and to pay
    B   I've been wanted and on paying
    C   I had been wanting and on paying
    D   I have wanted and to pay   **Answer**

30. The work has taken ___ time to complete than the ___ time.

    A   less and first
    B   fewer than and last
    C   few and first
    D   less than and last   **Answer**

31. I thought ___ left the keys in the car but realized this was something I ___ normally do.

   A   its and won't
   B   I'd and wouldn't
   C   I've and who's
   D   I'm and weren't   **Answer**

32. Half the team gave the proposal their ___ support while the rest thought it a ___ .

   A   un-conditional and nonstarter
   B   unconditional and nonstarter
   C   un-condiditional and nonstarter
   D   unconditional and non-starter   **Answer**

33. As soon as she finishes her ___ assignment she will be let ___ on the next one.

   A   last and lose
   B   latest and loose
   C   late and lose
   D   later and loose   **Answer**

34. I don't expect to get it back and only placed the advert in the lost and found section of the newspaper as a matter of ___ but if anyone calls about the lost money please ___.

   A   principal and ask their number and I will call back
   B   moral correctness and ask them to call back
   C   principal and ask that they call back
   D   principle and take a number and I will call back

                                      Answer

35. Here is the site of the laboratory ___ it was invented and where pioneering work was undertaken ___ the discovery was put to its current day practical application.

   A   when and whose
   B   whereby and where
   C   where and whereby
   D   whose and when   **Answer**

End of test.

Practice test 4: Reading comprehension and critical reasoning

This test comprises eight passages and 40 questions, and you are allowed 45 minutes in which to attempt them. Each passage is followed by a series of questions or statements and it is your task to answer the question or statement by referring only to the contents of the passage. In every case you must indicate if the statement is true, false or if you cannot tell if the statement is true or false. To indicate your answer, write true, false or cannot tell in the answer box provided.

Work without interruption and complete the test in one continuous period.

If you do not know the answer to a question then it is worth guessing, but only as a last resort.

Remember that to do well in a test you have to try hard.

Do not turn the page until you are ready to begin.

Passage 1

India is fast becoming the world's biggest supplier of services to Europe and the United States. It used to be thought that services had to be delivered in the same country as the customer because they required staff to be near their clients. In the world of outsourcing, telesales and internet purchasing this is no longer the case and service providers in Europe and the United States have struggled to compete because of the regulatory burden and high wages. Now India has its sights on winning business in the sectors of banking, finance, accountancy and law. It seems that very little can be done to stop European and US jobs in these industries going the same way as so many manufacturing jobs and migrating to the huge, English speaking, highly educated and low wage Indian workforce.

1. The passage promotes the view that India is making inroads into new markets that were once considered safe from overseas competition.

    True
    False
    Cannot tell   **Answer** [   ]

2. It is asserted in the passage that service providers in Europe and the United States are put at a disadvantage because of regulatory burdens and high wages.

    True
    False
    Cannot tell   **Answer** [   ]

3. The passage suggests that India's economic growth is unsustainable.

    True
    False
    Cannot tell   **Answer** [   ]

4.   The loss of manufacturing jobs is less of a worry than the loss of jobs in the service industries.

True
False
Cannot tell   **Answer**

5.   The author would not agree that there is little we can do to stop European and US jobs in banking, finance, accountancy and law being lost to India.

True
False
Cannot tell   **Answer**

Passage 2

No trains, hardly any buses, everyone stranded unless they drive. This is the situation every year in Britain when the transport network closes over the Christmas break. Workers in hospitals, prisons, the police force and fire service must somehow find their way to work without public transport. Families divided by geography are forced to either drive or remain separated. Many low wage workers cannot afford the luxury of a long holiday break and so must find a way to get to work without public transport or suffer the financial consequences. No other European country closes its public transport over the Christmas period. The British authorities claim that if they ran a service it would not make a profit.

6.   The author considers the lack of transport over the Christmas break no more than an inconvenience.

True
False
Cannot tell   **Answer**

7. Workers in hospitals, prisons, the police force and fire service are not described in the passage as essential workers.

    True
    False
    Cannot tell   **Answer** [   ]

8. It can be inferred from the passage that Britain is unique in Europe for the lack of public transport over the Christmas period.

    True
    False
    Cannot tell   **Answer** [   ]

9. The authorities would run trains over the period if the government paid them to.

    True
    False
    Cannot tell   **Answer** [   ]

10. It can be inferred from the passage that transport providers run public transport in order to provide a service.

    True
    False
    Cannot tell   **Answer** [   ]

Passage 3

In 2007, 150 million people joined social network internet sites, a 400 per cent increase on the traffic in 2006. An energetic social networking industry has arrived but a business model has yet to emerge. The challenge for the industry is not how to attract users but how to make money. In particular they must work out how to generate income while reconciling the interests of the user, software developer and advertiser. The user and their social network of family and friends expect the service to be free and their privacy to be maintained. Software developers provide games and photo slideshows and in return want to promote other products and services to users. The site owner obviously wants to make money, so targets advertisers willing to pay in order to market to the millions of users. Friction is inevitable as the industry experiments with ways to realize revenue.

11. Facebook is the name of a social networking site.

    True
    False
    Cannot tell   **Answer** [   ]

12. In the passage the interests of three separate groups are discussed.

    True
    False
    Cannot tell   **Answer** [   ]

13. While the passage states that a business model has yet to emerge it is clear from the passage that it is expected that revenue will be provided by advertisers.

    True
    False
    Cannot tell   **Answer** [   ]

14. A synonym of energetic is vigorous.

    True
    False
    Cannot tell   **Answer** [ ]

15. The tone of the passage suggests that despite the challenges, internet social networking sites are here to stay.

    True
    False
    Cannot tell   **Answer** [ ]

Passage 4

Current levels of domestic inflation make it a lot easier for the government of China to accept a stronger domestic currency (the Yuan). Until recently, the government was concerned that strengthening the Yuan would lead to domestic deflation. Chinese trade surpluses are resulting in the accumulation of foreign exchange reserves equal to $1 billion a day. Trading partners, especially the United States, are keen to see a stronger Yuan, hoping that it will pull back the level of trade surplus. Imported commodities – the raw materials necessary for China's manufacturing industry – have become far more expensive and a stronger Yuan will help offset some of these increases.

16. Deflation and surplus are antonyms.
    True
    False
    Cannot tell   **Answer** [ ]

17. Two potential advantages of a stronger Yuan are described in the passage.

    True
    False
    Cannot tell   **Answer**

18. If it were the case that domestic inflation in China stood at over 5 per cent, then the Chinese government would have greater concerns over the domestic effects of a stronger Yuan.

    True
    False
    Cannot tell   **Answer**

19. The author expects the reader to know that the domestic currency of China is called the Yuan.

    True
    False
    Cannot tell   **Answer**

20. It is clear from the passage that the Yuan value has been allowed to rise.

    True
    False
    Cannot tell   **Answer**

Passage 5

Environmental scientists rarely look back to see if their old forecasts were accurate and in some instances they offer such long-term predictions that we will all be dead long before the validity or falsehood of their calculations is established. In the 1970s scientists warned that a nuclear war, large meteorite strike or series of big volcanic eruptions could trigger a cooling of the world and the dawn of a new ice age. In the 1980s they warned of a recently discovered hole in the ozone layer and of the catastrophic effects that would follow if it was to grow. Today scientists link the burning of fossil fuels to increased concentrations of carbon dioxide and predict that the ice sheets of Antarctica will melt within 1,000 years, causing sea levels to rise six metres, drowning vast tracts of land and whole communities. These predictions are alarming, newsworthy and influence public behaviour but given that in practice they are not verified or impossible to verify we must question if are they based on good scientific methods.

21. In the passage the author states that he does not accept that burning fossil fuels is causing an increase in concentrations of carbon dioxide.

    True
    False
    Cannot tell   **Answer**

22. The passage does not detail occasions when the environmental scientists' forecasts were proved to be false.

    True
    False
    Cannot tell   **Answer**

23. The passage is written from the standpoint that foretelling the future is difficult and when people try to do it they are nearly always wrong.

    True
    False
    Cannot tell   **Answer**

24. The experiences of the author make him sceptical of how environmental forecasting is being used.

    True
    False
    Cannot tell   **Answer**

25. A synonym of verified is unproven.

    True
    False
    Cannot tell   **Answer**

Passage 6

People should buy more fresh food that they then use to prepare proper meals and whenever possible buy locally produced food from local shops. Instead we treat food like fuel. We seek out the most convenient, which is often processed industrially and supplied by multinationals and this has consequences for both public health and the environment. We eat it in a hurry and on the move rather than together around a table. Pre-packed meals are wasteful because of all the packaging and distribution involved. People lack the skills and knowledge needed to turn back to good food.

26. The main point in the passage is that we treat food like fuel and seek out the cheapest and most convenient.

    True
    False
    Cannot tell   **Answer** [   ]

27. The most convenient food is usually also the cheapest.

    True
    False
    Cannot tell   **Answer** [   ]

28. By 'good food' the author means industrially produced meals.

    True
    False
    Cannot tell   **Answer** [   ]

29. Many industrially produced meals contain too much fat and sugar giving rise to obesity and high blood pressure. This is the sort of thing the author is implying when he writes that industrially produced food has consequences for public health.

    True
    False
    Cannot tell   **Answer** [   ]

30. The view that we do not respect food enough is consistent with the position adopted by the author in the passage.

    True
    False
    Cannot tell   **Answer** [   ]

Passage 7

A US survey of how children spend their pocket money found that a sizeable amount of it is spent on sweets, snacks and fizzy drinks. The study asked the children to keep a diary of their purchases over a two-year period. On average the children spent $23 a week and over a third of this was spent on sugary and fatty foods and drinks. The survey found marked differences in spending trends in sex and age. Boys spent less on clothes, shoes and toiletries and more on games, computer-related items and hobbies. The children spent equal sums on mobile phones and activities and objects that could be classed as educational. Both sexes spent equal amounts on music but boys spent more on sporting activities.

31. It can be inferred from the information given that the survey was based on the responses of 4,000 children.

    True
    False
    Cannot tell   **Answer** [   ]

32. We can tell from the information given that the sizeable amount spent on sweets, snacks and fizzy drinks amounted to less than half the children's total pocket money.

    True
    False
    Cannot tell   **Answer** [   ]

33. The biggest spenders in the survey were children aged 13 to 15 years.

    True
    False
    Cannot tell   **Answer** [   ]

34. Study is a synonym of survey.

True
False
Cannot tell   **Answer**

35. The author of the passage is describing attempts to solve a problem.

True
False
Cannot tell   **Answer**

Passage 8

Our international institutions and treaties have failed to move with the times. They were formed to provide a system through which to tackle common threats while protecting national interests. But interdependence has advanced beyond anything imagined then and in recent times the global institutions have proved totally powerless at providing successful global authority. All too often efforts to address the many common challenges are pulled down by narrow national interests.

36. The passage is concerned with our collective failure to protect the environment from the damage wreaked by individual companies and nations.

True
False
Cannot tell   **Answer**

37. The passage does not touch on potential solutions, only the problem of ineffectual global governance.

    True
    False
    Cannot tell   **Answer** [   ]

38. An entirely new system of global governance is required to address the many common global challenges.

    True
    False
    Cannot tell   **Answer** [   ]

39. In the passage, the failure to tackle common threats is attributed to national interests.

    True
    False
    Cannot tell   **Answer** [   ]

40. In the passage the term interdependence is explained.

    True
    False
    Cannot tell   **Answer** [   ]

End of test.

7

Answers, explanations and interpretations of your score

Chapter 2: 150 warm-up questions

Find the new word

1. move
   Explanation: the word move is formed by the last two letters in Eskimo and the first two letters in vertical.

2. some
   Explanation: the last two letters of espresso and the first two letters of message form the word some.

3. idea
   Explanation: an abstract noun names something that we cannot see or touch such as an idea.

4. mast
   Explanation: the last three letters of Christmas and the first letter of talent spell mast.

5. tart

   Explanation: the last three letters in Eurostar and the first letter in tennis spell tart.

6. should

   Explanation: a conditional is a term that expresses a condition. Examples are would and if as well as should.

7. easy

   Explanation: the last letter of humble and the first three letters of asylum spell easy.

8. zero

   Explanation: the last two letters of exorcize and the first two letters of round spell zero.

9. glass

   Explanation: the last letter of evening and the first four letters of lasso spell glass.

10. when

    Explanation: a conjunction is a word that forms a link between two clauses. In this case the word 'when' serves to link the clause that describes the relaxing bath with the event of the phone ringing.

11. tell

    Explanation: the last two letters of evaporate and the first two letters of Lloyd spell tell.

12. star

    Explanation: the last two letters of frost and the first two of archery spell star.

13. older

    Explanation: a comparative word or phrase draws a comparison between things and attributes one with the higher extent. In the question the sentence is making a comparison between the age of the speaker and his sister and the word 'older' identifies which of them is greatest in age.

14. will

    Explanation: the last letter of curfew and the first three letters of illegal spell will.

15. stir or ants

    Explanation: the last two letters of outpost and the first two of irritant spell stir; the last three letters of irritant and the first letter of spangle spell ants.

16. gently

    Explanation: an adverb is a word or phrase that qualifies or modifies. The word 'gently' in the sentence tells us that he carefully fitted the picture and this modifies or adds to our understanding of what was happening.

17. goat

    Explanation: the last two letters in flamingo and the first two in attack spell goat.

18. here

    Explanation: the last three letters in feather and the first letter in evolve spell here.

19. You've

    Explanation: a contraction is a short form of a subject and (auxiliary) verb. The suggested answers are the shortened forms of you are, you have, you will and you had or you would.

20. rich

    Explanation: the last three letters of electric and the first letter of horrid spell rich.

21. swarm

    Explanation: a noun names something or someone and a collective noun names a group of things. The collective name for a group of bees is a swarm.

22. both

    Explanation: the last two letters of gumbo and the first two of thorn spell both.

23. rasp

    Explanation: the last two letters of okra and the first two of sparrow spell rasp.

24. sick

    Explanation: the last three letters of forensic and the first letter of knowledge spell sick.

25. erupting

    Explanation: a verb describes an action and an active verb is one that is described as occurring rather than as having occurred.

26. hero

    Explanation: the last letter of though and the first three of erode spell hero.

27. wait

    Explanation: the last two letters of fatwa and the first two of itinerary spell wait.

28. than or malt

    Explanation: the last two letters of froth and the first two of animal spell than; the last three letters of animal and the first letter of tourist spell malt.

29. game

    Explanation: the last letter of dangling and the first three letters of amendment spell game.

30. 3

    Explanation: a concrete noun names something that we can see or touch and in the sentence the words milk, sugar and coffee are concrete nouns.

31. dawn

    Explanation: the last letter of divided and the first three of awning spell dawn.

32. cult

Explanation: the last letter of specific and the first three of ultrasound spell cult.

33. all of them

Explanation: a countable noun is one that can be used correctly in the plural form, ie horse and horses, and can be given the article a/an.

34. gyro

Explanation: the last two letters of philology and the first two of rotund spell gyro.

35. tale

Explanation: the last three letters of experimental and the first letter in eruption spell tale.

36. impossible

Explanation: an adjective names an attribute of someone or something and that the test is almost impossible is an attribute of it.

37. self

Explanation: the last three letters of diesel and the first letter of fizzle spell self.

38. came

Explanation: the last two letters of harmonica and the first two letters of method spell came.

39. dash

Explanation: the last two letters of Canada and the first two letters of shackle spell dash.

40. this and that

Explanation: 'this' and 'that' are demonstrative articles as they are used to illustrate something. 'The' is a definite article rather than a demonstrative article.

41. kite or tent

    Explanation: the last three letters of skit and the first letter of entitle spell kite; the last letter of skit and the first three letters of entitle spell tent.

42. bark or ages

    Explanation: the last three letters of sandbar and the first letter of kitchen spell bark; the last three letters of barrage and the first letter of sandbar spell ages.

43. would and if

    Explanation: a conditional expression adds a condition to something. Take the sentence, 'I will give all my money to charity.' It is unconditional. Compare it with, 'I should give all my money to charity' and, 'I would give all my money to charity.'

44. shot

    Explanation: the last two letters of flush and the first two of otherwise spell shot.

45. toil

    Explanation: the last letter in toast and the first three in oilfield spell toil.

46. mess

    Explanation: the last letter in metabolism and the first three in essence spell mess.

47. test, bone or nest

    Explanation: the last two letters of estate and the first two of stigma spell test; the last three letters of carbon and the first letter of estate spell bone; the last letter of carbon and the first three letters of estate spell nest.

48. stew

    Explanation: the last two letters of dentist and the first two of ewe spell stew.

49. deaf

    Explanation: the last three letters of idea and the first letter of fear spell deaf.

50. demo

    Explanation: the last letter of dead and the first three of emotional spell demo.

Word link – opposites

51. A, serious

    Explanation: shallow normally means the opposite of deep but we also say of a conversation that it is shallow meaning that it is silly or frivolous. The opposite of a frivolous or shallow conversation would be a serious one.

52. C, telling

    Explanation: an active verb describes an action that is occurring; 'was told' is something that has already occurred while 'telling' is active in that it is described as occurring.

53. B, ignorance

    Explanation: the term understanding can mean a number of related things including knowledge of or expertise in something or familiarity or acquaintance with something. The opposite of this meaning is ignorance or being ill-informed.

54. C, entrance

    Explanation: we speak of the departure gate in an airport and the opposite of this is the entrance. The opposite of admit would be exclude not departure.

55. B, unify

    Explanation: divide can mean both separate and share-out; the opposite of the first of these meanings is to unify.

56. A, open

    Explanation: covert means secretive and the opposite is someone who is open about their intentions or actions.

57. 3

   Explanation: a concrete noun names something solid rather than abstract and in the sentence the words mountains, snow and peaks are concrete nouns.

58. A, general

   Explanation: intricate means detailed and the opposite is general. Something large can be intricate as can be something that is inexact.

59. 3, more enjoyable.

   Explanation: in the sentence it is the phrase more enjoyable that identifies the book as giving greater enjoyment than the film.

60. C, commoner

   Explanation: count can mean to arrive at the total but it is also a title of a member of the aristocracy and the opposite is a commoner – someone without title.

61. tomorrow

   Explanation: an adverb modifies the meaning of a sentence and the word tomorrow in this sentence adds to or modifies our understanding of when the flights will be booked

62. A, dishonest

   Explanation: if someone is honest it is said they are square or straight. It can also mean that they are boring. The opposite of honest is dishonest.

63. B, reasonable

   Explanation: steep can mean to saturate with a liquid or it can mean a steep incline. Another meaning and the one that applies here is when something is expensive it is said to be steep and the opposite of that is reasonable.

64. 4

   Explanation: the imperative form involves the giving of orders or making of suggestions. The others are examples of, 1 the future perfect, 2 hypothetical, 3 future continuous.

65. B, point

    Explanation: a knife is blunt if it has lost its point or edge; to be blunt is also to be forthright in your opinions.

66. C, adore

    Explanation: to loathe, deplore or abhor all mean to dislike strongly; adore means to like a lot so is the opposite.

67. 5, we are

68. B, raise

    Explanation: to ruin something means to destroy or spoil it. To mar something means to spoil it and to undo something can mean to ruin it. To raise something would be the opposite to ruin.

69. C, subservient

    Explanation: ascendant means to hold a position of status and subservient means to be at a lower status.

70. A, eat

    Explanation: fast can mean go fast or tighten; it can also mean to abstain from eating.

71. A, susceptible

    Explanation: something is resistant if it is unsusceptible or immune; the opposite is susceptible.

72. B, involve

    Explanation: to invoke means to appeal or summon, to invite means to ask while involve means to include and is the opposite of exclude.

73. B, depress

    Explanation: animate means to excite or give the appearance of life. The opposite would be to depress.

74. C, increase

    Explanation: commute means to travel but also to reduce something. The opposite to this second meaning is increase.

75. team

Explanation: a noun names something or someone and a collective noun names a group of things or people; the name of a group of footballers is a team.

76. A, denial

Explanation: a concession is a compromise or something permitted, reduced or given up. The opposite is a denial of the request.

77. B, spotless

Explanation: defect can mean to be a traitor or to desert your position but it also means with fault and the opposite of this is faultless. The closest meaning to this in the suggested answers is spotless.

78. idea

Explanation: a countable noun is one that has a plural form, ie ideas, and can be given the article a/an: 'an idea'. We cannot have 'a water', etc; all the other examples are uncountable nouns.

79. A, central

Explanation: peripheral means marginal, secondary or incidental; the opposite is something central.

80. C, compliant

Explanation: intractable can refer to either a stubborn person or a problem that is hard to solve. In the case of the first of these meanings compliant is the opposite.

81. C, start

Explanation: to tail can mean to follow or in other words shadow and to fade away. It is also the end of something and the opposite of this meaning is the start.

82. C, spotless

Explanation: soil can mean the medium plants grow in and it also means made dirty or foul; its antonym is clean or spotless.

83. height

    Explanation: the name of something that we cannot touch or see is an abstract noun; height is a concept rather than something concrete like a mountain and this makes it abstract and its name an abstract noun.

84. C, withdraw

    Explanation: to tender something is to offer it and the opposite to this meaning is withdraw. Tender also means gentle or sympathetic.

85. B, thrifty

    Explanation: profligate means wasteful while profuse means abundant. The opposite of wasteful is thrifty or in other words careful.

86. B, abridge

    Explanation: elongate means to stretch or extend and the opposite of this is abridge, which means shorten.

87. 1, smaller

    Explanation: a comparative makes a comparison between the extent that two things have of a quality and identifies which has the most of that quality. But it does not identify something as having the maximum amount of a quality. For this reason smaller is a comparative but smallest is not. Braver would be a comparative but bravest is not.

88. C, wrong

    Explanation: orthodox means true or genuine and the opposite is wrong.

89. and

    Explanation: conjunctions make links between clauses and in the sentence the word 'and' serves to link the clause that I ate too much with the second clause that I felt unwell.

90. A, upright

    Explanation: prone can mean that something is likely or that something is laying flat. The opposite of this second meaning is upright.

91. B, tend

    Explanation: neglect means to fail to do something, to not look after or tend something.

92. C, finite

    Explanation: unlimited means limitless and the opposite is finite or with boundaries.

93. A, seldom

    Explanation: ceaselessly means always and the opposite is seldom or never.

94. 2

    Explanation: an adjective names an attribute or quality belonging to something or someone. In the sentence the words cheeky and cheerful are adjectives.

95. B, outmoded

    Explanation: contemporary means modern, of this time, and the opposite is outmoded or old fashioned.

96. A, boom

    Explanation: to slump is to sit down exhausted; a slump is an economic decline the opposite of which is an economic boom.

97. C, borrow

    Explanation: if you lend something they borrow it. These are opposites.

98. A, certainty

    Explanation: possibly means something may happen; certainty means it will happen. In this respect they are opposites.

99. B, differ

    Explanation: if two things resemble one another they have qualities in common; the opposite of this is when two things differ.

100. A, euphoric

    Explanation: euphoric means very happy, the opposite of miserable. Effusive means enthusiastic and eclectic means comprehensive.

Word link – synonyms

101. A, alienate
Explanation: to isolate is to separate and another way of saying this is alienate.

102. C, ancestry
Explanation: lineage means descent from our forefathers and another term for this is ancestry.

103. all of them
Explanation: the superlative form of adjectives ends in 'est' or is structured 'most…'.

104. C, prolific
Explanation: prolong means lengthen and propagate means cultivate, while prolific is a synonym of abundant.

105. B, vocalize
Explanation: utter can mean speak or total; a synonym of the first of these meanings is vocalize.

106. once
Explanation: an adverb qualifies or modifies our understanding of something and the word once in this sentence qualifies our understanding of the fact that they had visited the city before – but only once.

107. A, banal
Explanation: banal means that something is ordinary, stale and overdone. Baleful means menacing.

108. 3, won't

109. B, cartoon
Explanation: a caricature is a funny portrait or description often used in newspapers or on film as cartoons. A criticism is an expression of disproval while a concoction is something made up.

110. A, weaken

    Explanation: to debilitate something is to incapacitate it or break it.

111. if

    Explanation: 'if' is the conditional expression in the sentence. Without it the sentence would assert that the weather is without doubt going to be bad. Adding the conditional expression alters the sense to the possibility of bad weather.

112. C, obtain

    Explanation: to elicit something is to obtain or draw out a response.

113. family

    Explanation: nouns name things or people and collective nouns name a group; the name for relatives of someone is their family.

114. B, amenity

    Explanation: we talk of toilet facilities or facilities for people with special needs and these are types of amenity.

115. A, comprehensive

    Explanation: something that is general is widespread, mixed or customary.

116. C, ensue

    Explanation: occur means to happen or take place and ensue has a similar meaning, namely to follow or arise.

117. A, perception

    Explanation: perception is to become aware of something and we say we have insight if we perceive something, especially if we perceive it intuitively.

118. 2

    Explanation: a concrete noun is the name of something concrete rather than something abstract. Car park and vehicles are the two concrete nouns in this sentence (where we leave vehicles is a car park so we count it as one concrete noun not two, car and park).

119. C, class

Explanation: the word type has a number of meanings one of which is the classification of something into kinds or types called class, set or species.

120. none of these

Explanation: we say, for example, aren't you coming to mean you are not coming, but 'am not' does not have a contraction.

121. B, ordinarily

Explanation: usually means as a rule, normally, and a synonym is ordinarily. A synonym of actually is seriously and one of completely is totally.

122. A, same

Explanation: alike means similar. Same can mean identical – we share the same birthday – but it also means similar or alike: the girls are very alike. Twins are offspring born at the same birth. Identical (and twin) mean indistinguishable.

123. because

Explanation: a conjunction joins two clauses together. Commonly used conjunctions are and, but, although and if, to name but a few.

124. C, principal

Explanation: principle signifies theory or belief while predominance means majority. Principal means foremost or most important.

125. A, over

Explanation: we sometimes say something is over when it has gone. More signifies extra and here means now or at that time.

126. B, first

Explanation: best, first and prime can all signify the best of something but only first can also mean the earliest.

127. A, signify

    Explanation: the word mean can stand for all three of these suggested answers. The answer is A however because in this instance the word is used as a verb. In the case of midpoint, mean is used as a noun; when it stands for being miserly it is used as an adjective.

128. C, favourable

    Explanation: advantageous means of benefit or valuable, reasonable means realistic and fair means just. Only favourable signifies the advantage also signified by the term advantageous.

129. B, observe

    Explanation: we say for example that 'he eyed the couple suspiciously', meaning watched or observed.

130. A, doubt

    Explanation: to be uncertain is to be unsure about something or have doubt. To disbelieve is to hold that something is untrue, while suspicion means mistrust.

131. C, come

    Explanation: to approach means to come near or come close. When we want someone to approach we same 'come'. Progress means develop or grow.

132. B, economical

    Explanation: low-cost means cheap or economical; it does not mean cheep, which is a word used to describe bird song.

133. C, exist

    Explanation: to be means to exist; happening means to occur.

134. mathematics

    Explanation: an abstract noun is the name of a concept rather than something real. The study of any subject is abstract and the name of a subject is an abstract noun.

135. A, as

   Explanation: a synonym of since is as; another is because. We can say 'as you asked', 'because you asked', 'since you asked'.

136. 5

   Explanation: an adjective names an attribute or quality of something or someone. In the sentence the following words are adjectives: blue, technical, advanced, yellow and next.

137. C, mistaken

   Explanation: something fallacious is mistaken or wrong.

138. B, dual

   Explanation: we say for example dual carriageway to indicate that there are two lanes. We say double crossed to suggest betrayal and double dealing to suggest duplicity, but we would not say just double.

139. A, use

   Explanation: we say that ships ply the seas and mean that they work or use them. Ply can also mean layer.

140. B, rubbish

   Explanation: when used as a noun, refuse means waste or rubbish; when used as a verb it means to decline or withhold.

141. A, specific

   Explanation: to be definite means to state clearly, in other words to be specific.

142. C, indistinct

   Explanation: something can look or sound faint and you can feel faint. It means weak, dim or indistinct. If you feel sick it can involve you feeling faint but they are not synonymous.

143. B, string

   Explanation: a sequence is the order in which related things are arranged. Another way to describe a sequence is to say a string.

144. calling

    Explanation: an active verb describes an action that is taking place. The term swimming can be an active verb; in the context of the sentence it is not a verb but names the swimming pool.

145. B, choose

    Explanation: to opt for something is to decide; both consider and ponder imply that a decision has not yet been made.

146. C, difficult

    Explanation: arduous means difficult while divergent means different and distinguish to tell apart.

147. B, ensure

    Explanation: ensure means make certain that something will or will not happen; ensue means result while entail means involve.

148. A, prove

    Explanation: to establish something can mean to inaugurate or prove.

149. C, close

    Explanation: as a verb intimate means proclaim or divulge; as an adjective it means close or cherished: 'they were intimate friends'.

150. Only 'dog' is countable

    Explanation: a countable noun is one that has a plural form and can be used with the article a/an. The other suggested answers are uncountable.

Chapter 3: 150 verbal reasoning questions

Synonyms and antonyms mixed up – this makes the questions harder

1. C, dull
   Explanation: the word dry has many meanings. It means the opposite of wet but we also use it when referring to emotions to mean indifferent and conversations to signify they are dull.

2. A, involvement
   Explanation: we can speak of a part of a whole (a fraction), a part or chapter of a book, the role or part someone plays in a show and in this instance the part or involvement someone has in a business deal or crime.

3. A, loose
   Explanation: fast can mean rapid and also secure; the antonym of this second meaning is loose.

4. B, not many
   Explanation: few means not many, some, but not lots. Few is used when something is countable. Less is not a synonym of few because we say less when we refer to uncountable nouns: 'there is less water in this bucket'.

5. C, profit
   Explanation: the antonym of loss is profit; saved is the antonym of lost.

6. C, end
   Explanation: dawn can mean day break but also beginning; the antonym of this second meaning is end.

7. B, last
   Explanation: continue means to carry on; its antonym is impede. Last when used as a verb also means continue; for example, 'the batteries lasted ages'.

8. A, given

   Explanation: the word go means leave; it also means given when we say for example, 'the old car will go to the scrap heap'.

9. A, discount

   Explanation: to ponder is to consider and the opposite is to discount or ignore.

10. B, delayed

    Explanation: if you got this question wrong then reread the question. It said, 'Which of the following is an antonym of...'. The antonym of instant is delayed.

11. C, remove

    Explanation: pull means drag or tug but also remove in the context of a dentist pulling a tooth or a TV channel pulling a programme.

12. A, subtract

    Explanation: to take something is to obtain or remove it. Another word for take (in the remove sense) is subtract.

13. C, original

    Explanation: the antonym of stale is original; its synonym is outdated or old. Impasse is the synonym of stalemate.

14. B, extremely

    Explanation: very means to a great extent; the antonym is slightly. We say very or extremely happy, very or really kind.

15. A, pliable

    Explanation: intransigent means inflexible and its antonym is pliable.

16. C, cope

    Explanation: deal means agreement, but we also say that we know how to deal with something, meaning cope with it.

17. B, realistic

    Explanation: idealistic means something perfect, as in an idea that may not work out in practice; synonyms are naive or optimistic.

18. C, conceal
   Explanation: exhibit means show and its antonym is to hide or conceal.

19. A, clinch
   Explanation: we close a door; meaning to shut it; he closed the meeting, meaning it ended; we close in on something, meaning we narrow the gap. We also say that we close a deal to mean that we clinched it or secured it.

20. B, express
   Explanation: put means place but it also means put across meaning; we express a view.

21. A, detailed
   Explanation: broad has many meanings including wide, comprehensive, obvious and pronounced. It also means general and the antonym of this meaning is detailed.

22. C, adjust
   Explanation: set has a number of meanings, one of which is position or adjust; for example, I set or adjust my watch.

23. B, absorb
   Explanation: emit means discard, give out or release and its antonym is absorb.

24. A, heterogeneous
   Explanation: uniform means regular or homogeneous; its antonym is heterogeneous or varied.

25. A, smooth
   Explanation: even means flat, uniform or smooth; the antonym is rough.

26. C, lack
   Explanation: have means own or possess and to lack something is the antonym of have.

27. B, conformist

    Explanation: A conformist or conventional person is the antonym of a maverick, who is a rebel.

28. C, all

    Explanation: all is a synonym of every, utmost means greatest, and possible likely.

29. A, fill

    Explanation: we say that he filled the vacant place, he occupied it. Vacate is the antonym of occupied.

30. B, cancel

    Explanation: to delete something you remove or cancel it; the antonym is add. Omit means forgot or overlooked.

31. C, timely

    Explanation: inopportune means ill-timed or inconvenient and its antonym is timely.

32. A, nevertheless

    Explanation: though means nevertheless when we say, for example, 'you may not like these though you are welcome to try one'. Idea would be a synonym of thought, not though, and rigorous would be a synonym of thorough not though.

33. B, cursory

    Explanation: thorough means exhaustive or careful; its opposite is superficial or cursory.

34. C, different

    Explanation: equal means the same or corresponding and its opposite is different.

35. B, equal

    Explanation: when something is unbiased it is balanced and people are treated equally.

36. A, enthusiastic

    Explanation: indifferent means impassive or dispassionate and its antonym is to be enthusiastic.

37. A, integer

    Explanation: a synonym of number is integer. Integrate means put together and integral means essential part.

38. C, improper

    Explanation: not done means not started or finished, and its synonym is incomplete, but it also means improper. We say, for example, that something is just not done, meaning it is improper.

39. B, complain

    Explanation: to acquiesce is to comply, to go along; the opposite is to complain.

40. B, barely

    Explanation: only can mean barely as in there was only just (barely) enough; it can also mean simply and lone. Plainly means clearly, not simply; lonely means feeling alone, so neither are synonyms of only.

41. A, unspecified

    Explanation: given means specified and its antonym is unspecified.

42. A, distinct

    Explanation: to say something is clear is to say it is obvious or distinct. Opaque is its antonym.

43. B, remote

    Explanation: adjacent means neighbouring and its opposite is remote.

44. C, note

    Explanation: if we jot something down we write or note it. If we jolt something we bump it.

45. A, restore

    Explanation: exacerbate means make worse and its antonym is restore or improve.

46. B, equip
    Explanation: to furnish is to provide or supply; to acquire something is to obtain it not supply it.

47. A, weaken
    Explanation: to tire is to grow tired or lose strength. Veer means turn.

48. C, provoke
    Explanation: conciliate means make peace and to provoke is the antonym of this.

49. B, natural
    Explanation: affected means to be artificial or to exaggerate; the opposite is to act naturally.

50. C, efficient
    Explanation: lean is to incline or bend; something is also said to be lean if it is efficient and leaves little waste. This meaning is derived from the description of meat with little fat as lean.

Word swap

51. is and thing

52. monkeys and mammals

53. seemingly and world's

54. so and or

55. area and island

56. about and by

57. racial and equal

58. 10 and world's

59. complex and framework

60. shape and matter

61. between and (the first) the

62. is and exists

63. businesses and mathematics

64. to and too

65. 12 and 2002

66. Britain and The

67. (second) billions and galaxies

68. practice and discoveries

69. has and of

70. where and (first) from

71. vinegar and juice

72. temperature and (first) weather

73. human and disorders

74. reveal and magnifies

75. equations and letters

76. oceans and solution

77. Earth's and Earth

78. grade and examinations

79. public and private

80. created and comprises

81. everyone and ourselves

82. are and however

83. its and the

84. degree and careers

85. life and lead

86. and (second) to and

87. health and illness

88. changes and describes

89. south and stretching

90. is and looks

91. monitor and produce

92. European and population

93. behind and involved

94. in and by

95. industrialized and reconsidered

96. us and we

97. government and citizens

98. elderly and middle

99. ball and school

100. other and energy

Sentence sequence

101. C, B, D, A

102. B, D, A, C

103. C, A, D, B

104. B, D, C, A

105. C, B, A, D

106. B, D, C, A

107. D, A, C, B

108. A, C, B, D

109. D, B, C, A

110. A, C, B, D

111. C, D, A, B

112. C, B, D, A

113. A, C, D, B

114. C, A, D, B

115. C, A, B, D

116. C, A, B, D

117. C, A, D, B

118. D, A, C, B

119. C, B, D, A

120. B, C, D, A

121. D, C, B, A

122. C, A, D, B

123. B, C, D, A

124. A, C, D, B

125. C, B, A, D

126. D, C, B, A

127. B, A, C, D

128. C, D, B, A

129. B, A, D, C

130. B, A, D, C

131. C, D, A, B

132. B, D, C, A

133. A, D, B, C

134. B, D, A, C

135. C, A, D, B

136. B, A, C, D

137. D, A, C, B

138. D, C, B, A

139. B, C, D, A

140. D, C, B, A

141. B, D, C, A

142. D, C, B, A

143. B, C, A, D

144. C, A, D, B

145. B, C, A, D

146. D, A, C, B

147. C, B, D, A

148. B, D, C, A

149. D, A, B, C

150. A, C, B, D

Chapter 4: 150 English usage questions

1. A, of
    Explanation: we say consists of; a common error is to say from.

2. C, on
    Explanation: we congratulate on something, for example birthdays, weddings and successes.

3. B, in and into
    Explanation: we divide things in half but divide something into parts.

4. D, at and in
    Explanation: we say quick at something but weak in something.

5. A, of and from
    Explanation: we correctly say independent of and independence from something.

6. B, to
    Explanation: we say opposite to, or in another context opposite of, but not opposite from or for.

7. D, by and for
    Explanation: we say that we pass by something and play for a team.

8. C, at and on
    Explanation: we sit at a table but on a chair. It is possible to sit on a table but to say she sat on the table is an unlikely scenario and we can infer it is not the intended answer to the question.

9. D, with
    Explanation: we say covered with or in, but not by.

10. A, on and on
    Explanation: we say on horse-back and on foot, but by land and sea, by train or plane.

11. B, in and on
    Explanation: to confide means to tell a secret to someone. We confide in not to someone, but we can say 'we confide something to.'

12. C, from
    Explanation: we say different from but similar to; a common error is to say different than.

13. B, of
    Explanation: we correctly say be careful with or about something, but we say take care of something.

14. A, to and in
    Explanation: the correct prepositions are accustomed to and absorbed in.

15. C, at and at
    Explanation: we say we are angry at something and with people or animals; we arrive at not to a meeting or home.

16. A, of and with
    Explanation: we correctly say was full of not with, but we do say filled with.

17. C, with and on
    Explanation: we say persist with or persist in, but not insist with.

18. B, with and to
    Explanation: we say something is popular with and that we prefer something to something else.

19. B, by and at
    Explanation: we can correctly say astonished at or by something, but we can correctly only say surprised at something.

20. C, of
    Explanation: we say composed of something; a common error is to say composed from.

21. B, of and for
    Explanation: we say cured of something and the cure for something.

22. D, of and of

Explanation: for both afraid and accused the correct prepositions is of.

23. C, about and it

Explanation: we can correctly say we are disappointed in, with or about something but not from something. We would say regretted it and not repeat 'his performance'.

24. C, of and to

Explanation: we say an exception of something or someone but an exception to the rule, etc.

25. C, about

Explanation: we correctly say glad about something and glad of the help.

26. A, about and of

Explanation: when making a general point we say warned about but when we refer to some specific thing we use the form warned of.

27. D, of and about

Explanation: we say we are ashamed of something and anxious about it.

28. D, of and to

Explanation: we correctly say we are tired of walking, or we can structure the phrase as tired from the walk; we tie a string to something not on it.

29. B, with

Explanation: we say he is writing with a black pen or he completed the form in black ink.

30. C, going and going

Explanation: going and not go are the correct prepositions with prevented and insisted.

31. B, about and at

Explanation: the correct preposition for anxious is about, and we say shooting at not against something. It is also correct to say shooting [no word needed] a living creature but suggested answer D is incorrect because it is wrong to say anxious for shooting.

32. B, talking and working

    Explanation: we can say correctly both prefer to talk or talking, but after the preposition 'instead', we say working not work.

33. A, speak and to master

    Explanation: after can we use the infinitive without the to. So the correct answer is can speak and struggled to master.

34. C, go and went

    Explanation: after did the correct tense when speaking in the past tense is the infinitive.

35. A, working and getting

    Explanation: we use working and getting with the prepositions tired and used.

36. C, hear and love

    Explanation: when a verb refers to a state such as to love or to hear, rather than an action, then we use the infinitive form.

37. B, was

    Explanation: the subordinate clause, 'what she was saying', should be in the same tense as the main clause of the sentence.

38. D, get and getting

    Explanation: in the example of getting up early in the summer we use the infinitive form to get, but in the case of how we feel in winter, we use the form getting with the preposition used.

39. D, could and was

    Explanation: Jane said is the past simple tense so we use could rather than can and was rather than is.

40. B, he cycled

    Explanation: we use the simple past tense to describe something in the past that frequently happened.

41. A, are going
    Explanation: we use the present continuous form when we refer to a future event that is very likely to happen.

42. D, had already finished and arrived
    Explanation: we express the action that completes first in the past perfect tense and we express the second action in the past tense.

43. C she
    Explanation: in English few objects are given a gender; ships and boats are exceptions. Notice that the sentence reads '…is', so we do not use the abbreviations that's and it's.

44. B, door of the car
    Explanation: strictly speaking it is only correct to use the structure, 'the … of the …'; however, you will often hear people omitting 'the …of the …', even through it is incorrect.

45. A, refused
    Explanation: the tense in the verb to ask is in the past so we keep this tense throughout the statement.

46. C, I
    Explanation: in conversation you will often hear people say me rather than I when referring to themselves as the object, but this is incorrect.

47. D, who
    Explanation: who, whose and which are reflective pronouns but we use who and whose to refer to people and which to refer to animals or things.

48. A, themselves
    Explanation: the correct form of the reflective pronoun is themselves not theirselves or thereselves.

49. B, another
    Explanation: another means an other but it is written as another and is incorrect if you write 'an other' when meaning more of the same.

50. C, either

    Explanation: when we refer to two items we say either; if more than two we say any. One is wrong because the question asks if '…' of them *are* good.

51. C, twice and greatest

    Explanation: when comparing two things we use the superlative form greatest or smallest, not greater or smaller; in the context of the question we say once or twice rather than one time or two times.

52. C, One and in

    Explanation: when we refer to a specific day or part of a day we say one day or one afternoon, and we say that we work in the rain not under it.

53. D, The girl was afraid of the dog

    Explanation: a preposition identifies a relationship between a noun and a subject; of is a preposition in afraid of.

54. B, and and that

    Explanation: from the incomplete sentence we can infer that the writer likes both blue and green and does not mean that he likes either blue or green. We can say correctly the reason is that they make me feel calm or because they make me feel calm, but it is wrong to say the reason is because they make me feel calm.

55. D, the and in

    Explanation: we say we entered the room but took part in a discussion.

56. C is incorrect

    Explanation: we can correctly say that someone is 14 (or any number of years), 14 years of age and 14 years old, but it is incomplete to say 14 years.

57. D, nor

    Explanation: when we say neither the correct correlation is nor.

58. B, but

    Explanation: conjunctions link parts of a sentence; there are many examples including but, because, and, and or.

59. A, between

    Explanation: when there are two people as is the case in the sentence then we say between. When there are more than two we say among or amongst.

60. C, the

    Explanation: in this instance 'the' is correct because the boat is the only one for sale. We would use a boat or an apple when referring to boats or apples in general or when the particular boat or apple was not specified.

61. A, Neither and either

    Explanation: the question requires the negative form 'neither ... either'. 'Both ... either' is wrong because Jane did not pass.

62. B, do

    Explanation: the infinitive form is the basic form of verbs: to do, to eat, to play.

63. D, might

    Explanation: we use might in the past tense when the outcome has been decided but we do not know what it is, and may when the outcome is still undecided.

64. A, he or she

    Explanation: the sentence starts with the singular each child, so the pronoun must also be expressed in the singular.

65. C, two

    Explanation: the grandmother and a boy are referred to in the sentence. You can tell this from the fact that the term boy is expressed in the singular possessive boy's rather than the plural boys'.

66. B [no word needed]

    Explanation: we do not add adverbs to adjectives such as unique because they are absolute and cannot be modified. If something is unique it cannot be more or less unique.

67. C, we will be

    Explanation: only C can be used to express a future event (an event that has not yet occurred).

68. D, biggest

    Explanation: when something is unique like the biggest ever then we use the superlative form. Descriptive adjectives such as big or biggish are used to draw a comparison.

69. C, lay

    Explanation: lay is the past tense form of lie (to recline); laid is the past tense form of lay (as in I lay the table for dinner); to lie is to tell a mistruth.

70. D, is

    Explanation: the subject is a singular – the interesting thing – so we correctly say, is the many ways (not are the many ways).

71. B, there're

    Explanation: the chocolates are plural (two are left) so the clause must begin with the plural there are, or its abbreviation there're.

72. D, thinking

    Explanation: verbs describe actions such as thinking, deciding, laughing and so on.

73. D, begun

    Explanation: to begin is an irregular verb and the past form is begun.

74. B, who

    Explanation: generally speaking we use who when the subject is identified as a particular person and that when we are referring to a group of people.

75. A, less and fewer

    Explanation: pronouns such as less and little are only used to quantify uncountable nouns such as fat or salt. In the case of countable nouns such as calories we use a pronoun such as fewer.

76. D, who
    Explanation: we say who when referring to a person and which or what when referring to an object or animal.

77. A, frozen
    Explanation: to freeze is an irregular verb and the past participle form is frozen.

78. B, besides
    Explanation: an adverb modifies the meaning of a phrase, besides means in addition to.

79. C, Are you finding
    Explanation: the sentence states 'all this noise' so we use the present continuous verb form 'are you finding'. Suggested answers A and D are wrong because the sentence must form a question and these answers do not.

80. A, was driving
    Explanation: when referring to an event that takes a long time to complete and continued up to or beyond an identified point in time we use the continuous form.

81. D, will affect
    Explanation: we use will when making a prediction. The downturn will affect the rest of the world is correct because the downturn will result in change (affect) rather than is the result of change (effect).

82. C, the
    Explanation: a determiner always precedes a noun and adds information; examples are the, my, that, a, an, every and most.

83. D, is going to
    Explanation: when we predict something and support the prediction with current evidence we say going to be rather than will. We use will when we predict something that does not require evidence, for example, 'I will go swimming.'

84. A, staying

    Explanation: in this instance the writer will use staying, the future continuous form, because he does not want to invite the person to stay but only establish if they intend to stay. To say will you stay with us again tonight is to invite the person.

85. B, the past participle

    Explanation: the basic verb is to go; its past participle is gone and the future participle is going.

86. A, You don't need to be

    Explanation: when something is a necessary condition we usually say have to,' but we can also say need to when referring to a necessity in general. C is wrong because the sentence requires the word 'be' to make sense.

87. C, has

    Explanation: the subject is singular a member of parliament so the tense of the verb must also be singular. Suggested answer A is wrong because the criticism had already occurred.

88. D, clothes shop, woman's face and computer keyboard

    Explanation: when we refer to things or parts of things and animals we use the construction noun + noun (computer keyboard); when we refer to people or parts of people we prefer the construction noun's + noun (woman's face); clothes shop is an exception.

89. C, an and an

    Explanation: before words beginning with a vowel sound we use an rather than a.

90. A, one and another

    Explanation: in many situations we can replace 'one' with 'an' or 'a' but not when we structure a sentence one … another.

91. D, children's
    Explanation: the apostrophe indicates that the school is that of the children. If the sentence referred to only one child then it should read child's school. Childrens is wrong because children is already the plural form so we cannot correctly add an s unless without an apostrophe.

92. C, clever
    Explanation: an adjective adds meaning to a noun; in this case the noun boy.

93. B, was and were
    Explanation: if we say all of or some of and the noun is uncountable then we use was; if the noun is countable and plural we use were. Notice that we never say moneys only money, but do say possessions.

94. C, women's and woman's
    Explanation: the singular form is woman and the plural form is women (the centre is for women); the apostrophe indicates possession.

95. D, one and other
    Explanation: when we construct a sentence in the form ... one ... other, we don't substitute a/an for one, but adhere to the form 'one ... other.'

96. D, an and a
    Explanation: we use an before words that begin with a vowel sound and hour has a silent 'h' so we say an hour.

97. D, any and any
    Explanation: when constructing a negative statement we use any or anything rather than some or something.

98. C, No
    Explanation: we rarely start a sentence with 'not any' but prefer to use 'no' or 'none'. In this context 'none' and 'not a' do not make a sensible sentence.

99. B, many
    Explanation: when we refer to number we say many thousands/millions and so on and do not use the structure 'lots' or 'lots of'.

100. C, every

    Explanation: after almost we say every not each; suggested answers B and D do not make sensible sentences.

101. A, fewer and less

    Explanation: in the case of uncountable nouns such as eating we use less and not few or fewer. In the case of countable nouns such as thin people we can use few and fewer but not less.

102. C, she

    Explanation: the subject is the woman collector, the collection of stamps is the object and the verb the act of collecting.

103. D, is

    Explanation: the subject of the sentence 'his favourite dessert' is singular so we use is rather than are. Of is wrong because it does not form a complete sentence.

104. B, that

    Explanation: after a noun it is incorrect to use what.

105. A, ones

    Explanation: rather than repeat the word stalls we can replace it with 'ones'. Stalls is plural so we use ones rather than one.

106. B, because it was

    Explanation: the sentence needs a connection between the two clauses and the correct one will indicate that the connection is a cause for them being hungry. Of the suggested answers only 'because it was' does this.

107. C, so

    Explanation: we do not normally repeat a clause but replace it in this instance with so or such, provided that the meaning remains clear. In this case the meaning does remain clear so it is correct to avoid repeating the clause. So is preferred to such because we do not normally end a sentence with such.

108. D, the eclipse of the moon
Explanation: eclipse means hide or overshadow. It is the moon that is hidden or overshadowed in this sentence and answers A–C suggest that it is the moon that is hiding or overshadowing something. Only D correctly identifies the moon as being overshadowed.

109. C, virtually
Explanation: impossible is an upgradeable adjective and so we can't use adverbs such as reasonably, hugely and very.

110. B, wide and theirs
Explanation: we say something is completely or wide open and the deal is theirs meaning the people involved; widely means common or commonly found.

111. A, not disappointed enough
Explanation: to means in the direction of or near; too here means very. Suggested answers B and D would make sense with too but not with to. Only A makes a sensible sentence.

112. D, here Wednesday
Explanation: the order in which we record adverbs is first the place and then the time or date.

113. C, drove quickly home and arrived in time for the party
Explanation: we order adverbs thus: method then mood, place and time. Only suggested answer C correctly follows this convention.

114. D, They could not agree
Explanation: we can correctly construct an affirmative sentence along the line of they agreed where to go on holiday, and the negative form they could not agree where to go on holiday. We can add the expression 'at no time' or 'not once' but we must do so by saying not once could they agree where to go on holiday or at no time could they agree where to go on holiday. Suggested answer B is wrong because the sentence is not a question (if it were meant to be a question it would end with a question mark).

115. B, very

Explanation: we can say that we very much enjoyed something or that we very much appreciated it but we do not say very much or much interesting; we prefer the structure very interesting.

116. A, While

Explanation: While is correct because it introduces the timing of the event without implying a cause. As or because imply that the car was stolen because the person was at work, which does not make much sense. B is wrong because it does not build a complete sentence.

117. B, With

Explanation: if we start a sentence with 'with' it can serve to provide a reason, in this case the reason for not opening the playground.

118. D, so

Explanation: we can begin a clause in a sentence with because, since, as, or so, and the words serve to define the relationship with the previous clause. In this instance so is correct as it links the arrival of the guest to the reason why help cannot be provided.

119. A, though

Explanation: we can end a sentence with though but not with although. Through (from one side to the other) and trough (depression or channel) are similarly structured words with entirely different meanings.

120. B, isn't running

Explanation: to make sense the sentence needs the present continuous isn't running; there is no such word as ranning as suggested in D.

121. C, does not do anything

Explanation: only C completes the sentence correctly; doesn't is the abbreviation for does not, so suggested answer D unnecessarily repeats the word not.

122. D, plan to do

    Explanation: the sentence is written in the present tense referring to the future and given the structure only suggested answer D results in a sensible sentence. Suggested answer A would be correct if the sentence asked what are your ___ tomorrow and B would be correct if it were structured what are you ___ tomorrow.

123. B, sole

    Explanation: the word soul means an immortal part of the body; the word sole can mean a type of fish, the only person, or a part of the foot or shoe.

124. C, was doing

    Explanation: the sentence requires the past continuous, was doing or started doing; stopped doing could be acceptable except for the 'but'.

125. A, have been

    Explanation: of the suggested answers only A, the present perfect continuous – have been – creates a correct sentence.

126. D, all my life

    Explanation: all my life is preferable; when describing for how long something has occurred we can use for and since, but we can also correctly leave them out.

127. C, since 1989

    Explanation: we use for and since to describe how long something has occurred for. In this instance since is correct because of the specific date of the last eclipse; for would be used if for example we wrote there hasn't been a total eclipse of the sun for years.

128. A, A and the

    Explanation: when we refer to something as typical of a type we use a/an; when we refer to something unique or specific we use the.

129. C, Did you hear

     Explanation: when an event occurs in the past and has concluded we use the past tense I heard, I saw; but we use did and have in the present perfect: did you hear, did you see. A and B are incorrect because we do not follow see or seen with about.

130. A, principal and principle

     Explanation: take care not to confuse principal and principle. In this context principal means the most important person and principle means moral behaviour.

131. D, don't have and have got

     Explanation: notice the but in the sentence: this implies a contradiction between the clauses so we can rule out suggested answers B and C which treat the clauses as if they are in agreement. We can identify D as correct because it is incorrect to say don't got, as in A.

132. B, stationary and stationery

     Explanation: don't confuse stationery and stationary. Stationery means pens and paper, etc, while stationary means at rest.

133. C, she never read a newspaper.

     Explanation: only suggested answer C is correctly constructed in the past tense. D is incorrect because the statement refers to a specific period of years in the past and not past years in general.

134. A, their and there

     Explanation: don't confuse their and there. There means in a place; their means belonging to a person or persons.

135. A, I don't think I will

     Explanation: the sentence starts with the clause I'm not hungry so suggested answers C and D are incorrect as they do not make a sensible sentence. A is correct because we can say 'I think' and 'I don't think' but not 'I think I don't.'

136. D, here and hear
     Explanation: don't confuse hear and here. Hear means to hear/sense something, while here means at this place.

137. B, chief and chef
     Explanation: don't confuse chief and chef. Chief means the person in charge while chef is the title of a professional cook.

138. C, They and their
     Explanation: they and them both refer to two or more people, but they is used to identify the people as the subject, while them identifies the people as the object of a sentence. We say their poor health to indicate that they suffer the poor health.

139. D, accepts and except
     Explanation: don't confuse except with accept. Except means not included while accept means to receive or agree with.

140. B, haven't been able
     Explanation: it is correct to say I can't cycle or cannot cycle, but incorrect to say I can't cycle recently. Instead we say haven't or have not been able to.

141. C, right and write
     Explanation: don't confuse right and write. Right means correct or on the right side; write means to put pen to paper.

142. A, dare not
     Explanation: we correctly say I know not to, and I understand not to, but we drop the 'to' in dare not. Daren't is the abbreviation of dare not, so D is wrong because of the repetition of not.

143. C, council and counselling
     Explanation: don't confuse council and counsel. Council means administrative body; counsel means to advise.

144. D, one needs to
     Explanation: we correctly say 'you need to' or more formally 'one needs to.'

145. D, access and excess

   Explanation: don't confuse access and excess. Excess means greater than or too much. Access means to enter somewhere.

146. C, coming

   Explanation: after get used we do not use the infinitive form to come but the verb+ing form, coming.

147. A, advise and advice

   Explanation: don't confuse advise and advice. Advise is a verb meaning to offer a recommendation; advice is a noun meaning the recommendation.

148. B, for a

   Explanation: you can say let's go to the restaurant to eat but we say go for a meal. We prefer 'to' when we refer to something we do.

149. A, too, to and two

   Explanation: don't confuse too, to and two. Two is a number, we use 'to' to introduce a person or thing, and too to mean more than desirable.

150. D, of both

   Explanation: to make sense the sentence needs of both. Neither and either incorrectly imply that we like neither or only one of the films.

Chapter 5: 100 true, false and cannot tell questions

Passage 1

1. False
   Explanation: the passage states that we must only taste weak solutions of acid but nothing is said about the acid in our stomachs other than it is hydrochloric acid and so it is false that we can infer that the acid in our stomach is weak.

2. False
   Explanation: the primary purpose of the passage is to describe the properties and uses of acids. One of these properties is that they taste sour.

3. True
   Explanation: the passage states both that strongly acidic solutions burn and that a car battery contains a strong solution of sulphuric acid. It is be inferred from the passage therefore that the acid in a car battery will burn our skin.

4. Cannot tell
   Explanation: the passage states that a bee sting contains an acid and makes no reference to what is contained in a wasp sting so we cannot tell if the statement is true or false.

5. False
   Explanation: it is true that lemon juice is sour tasting but it is not true that this is mentioned in the passage; in fact no examples of sour tasting things are mentioned.

Passage 2

6. True

   Explanation: the passage states that the excavations took place in the 19th century and the date of the first games, 1896, is given and also falls within that century.

7. True

   Explanation: the passage states that the original Olympic games were held near the shore of the Ionian sea and named after mount Olympus, located near the Aegean Sea hundreds of miles to the east.

8. False

   Explanation: the passage states that the ancient Greeks thought that the gods and goddesses lived on mount Olympus.

9. Cannot tell

   Explanation: although it is true that the winner of a competition on the modern Olympics receives a gold medal and the runners-up silver and bronze, this is not stated in the passage so the correct answer is cannot tell.

10. False

    Explanation: in the context of the passage Marathon refers to the site of a battle in ancient times between Greek and Persian armies.

Passage 3

11. False

    Explanation: the main theme of the passage is the inequality that exists between bright children from high and low income families.

12. Cannot tell

    Explanation: the passage does not provide a definition of high income household so we cannot know if the suggested amount is correct or not.

13. True

    Explanation: the passage states that 'it has always been known that bright children from low income households do less well academically than bright children from high income households'.

14. False

    Explanation: the passage states that a bright child from a low income household is far less likely to win a place at university than a bright child from a high income family. The author therefore is unlikely to agree that a bright child, even a very bright child, from a low income household is very likely to go to university.

15. False

    Explanation: the passage does not claim nor is it implied that no bright children from low income households go to university, only that bright children from low income households are far less likely to win a place at university than bright children from high income households. This is not affected by the fact that some bright children from low income households do go to university. Before the claim in the passage was weakened it would need to be established that as many or nearly as many bright children from low income households went to university as bright children from high income households.

Passage 4

16. False

    Explanation: the passage described a number of adaptations that make it possible for penguins to live both an aquatic life and a life in a cold climate. But solid bones are described as an adaptation for an aquatic life rather than the cold. They are described as stronger and less buoyant, helping the birds dive deep down to their prey.

17. True

    Explanation: the passage states that penguins are only found in the southern hemisphere and so it can be inferred that to see them in the wild you must go to the southern hemisphere.

18. Cannot tell

    Explanation: most of us know that there are other species of flightless bird but the passage does not provide information on whether or not penguins are uniquely flightless in the bird world. For this reason we must answer cannot tell.

19. False

    Explanation: the passage does not state that penguins lay a single egg only that the penguins that live on sheet ice in the Antarctic incubate a single egg on the top of their feet.

20. True

    Explanation: the passage describes what is extraordinary about penguins and so the sentiment of the passage can correctly be captured by the statement that penguins are an extraordinary family of birds.

Passage 5

21. False

    Explanation: the passage describes two occasions when Germany has been unified, once in 1871 and again in 1990.

22. False

    Explanation: the only point made in the passage linked to the break-up of Germany in 1945 was defeat in the two World Wars. This is one reason despite the fact that there were two wars.

23. Cannot tell

    Explanation: the subject of how a reunified Germany will prosper is not touched upon in the passage and cannot be inferred from anything contained in the passage.

24. True

    Explanation: the wall is mention in relation to the country's division in 1945 into East and West and in relation to the reunification of the country in 1990.

25. True

    Explanation: the passage states that the wall was built in 1945 and demolished in 1990, which is a period of 45 years.

Passage 6

26. False

    Explanation: the passage presents only one view on the subject and does not provide either a counter argument or an alternative perspective.

27. True

    Explanation: the final sentence of the passage states that it is only the beginning of the revolution that will circle the globe as access to the internet becomes more widespread. From this we can infer that when the passage was written access to the internet was not universal.

28. False

    Explanation: penultimate means last but one and the illustration of the sorts of things that people post is the third sentence from the end of the passage.

29. False

    Explanation: the response of the traditional media corporations to the challenge of the internet is not mentioned so is not touched upon.

30. Cannot tell

    Explanation: we find views of every kind on the internet: the good, the bad, the wrong and the plain bizarre but the passage does not provide any information on this point and so going only on what is contained in the passage we cannot know if this statement is true or false.

Passage 7

31. False

    Explanation: the principal subject is a description of the process of producing books in general, both paper and hardback.

32. True

    Explanation: the passage explains why paperback books carry a lower price. It states 'they are less expensive to manufacture than hardback books so they can be sold at a lower price'.

33. True

    Explanation: the passage describes the process involved in producing a book and is understandable by a general audience as it requires no specialist knowledge of publishing.

34. Cannot tell

    Explanation: the prominence or otherwise of the Penguin publishing house today is not mentioned in the passage nor can it be inferred from the passage, so the correct answer is cannot tell.

35. False

    Explanation: the passage states that 'editors and designers work on the manuscript and produce what is called the proof'.

Passage 8

36. False

    Explanation: we know from the passage that the Pacific is the largest of the oceans but we are not informed of the total number of oceans nor can this information be inferred from the passage.

37. Cannot tell

    Explanation: in the passage the Pacific is described as the greatest ocean and twice as large as the next biggest, the Atlantic, but the fraction of the world's oceans attributable to the Pacific is not stated in the passage nor can it be inferred from the passage.

38. True

    Explanation: the passage states that the Pacific 'harbours trenches 11,000m deep, which makes it the deepest of the oceans'. From this we can conclude that no other ocean contains a trench of this depth.

39. Cannot tell

    Explanation: the passage states that the Pacific stretches from the Arctic to the Antarctic but it does not say if it is possible to travel by ship from the Arctic to the Antarctic without leaving the ocean nor is it possible to infer this information from the passage.

40. True

    Explanation: sentiment means feeling and it is true that the passage is about the greatness of the Pacific ocean in terms of its size and its resources.

Passage 9

41. False

    Explanation: idiosyncrasies can mean unconventional behaviour but in the context of the passage it refers to all differences, both behavioural and physical.

42. Cannot tell

    Explanation: the passage states that 'were to think the unthinkable and allow genetic engineering of the human DNA'. By unthinkable the author could mean either unacceptable or technologically impossible. We, therefore, are unable to infer from the passage the author's view on the genetic engineering of human DNA.

43. False

    Explanation: the Human Genome Project is mentioned in relation to the mapping of the sequence for human DNA and providing a blueprint of the DNA shared by every person.

44. True

    Explanation: design is a synonym of blueprint.

45. False

    Explanation: the passage states that DNA comprises the chemical code that governs the construction and function of every cell in our body. But from this it is not possible to infer that DNA is contained in every cell.

Passage 10

46. True

    Explanation: the case made in the passage is that graduates face considerable competition for good jobs and are no longer guaranteed to get one. If it were in fact the case that on graduation the majority of graduates did find good jobs then it is true that this would weaken the case made in the passage.

47. True

    Explanation: the author writes that 'in law enforcement, public administration, nursing, catering, retail, construction and transport there are many highly paid roles'. He then goes on to give the example of airline pilots. It is reasonable to infer therefore that the author is of the view that this role is highly paid.

48. False

    Explanation: the passage states 'that a degree is no longer a guaranteed route into a good job' and from this we can infer that a degree was once considered a guaranteed route into a good job.

49. False

    Explanation: the passage states that many young people drift into university not knowing what they want to do. This is a reason for going to university but it is not a particularly positive one.

50. False

    Explanation: the passage does not provide a reason why a degree is not a route into a good job nor does it touch on the reason.

Passage 11

51. True

    Explanation: the passage states that a solid has both a definite shape and volume while a liquid has no fixed shape but a definite volume.

52. Cannot tell

   Explanation: the passage does not comment on what happens to a liquid when it is cooled and the result cannot be inferred from the passage either.

53. True

   Explanation: substance is a synonym of matter.

54. False

   Explanation: three reasons are given. The first is if the solid is plastic, the second if it is elastic (its shape is only lost momentarily in this instance), the third if the solid is brittle.

55. True

   Explanation: the main theme of the passage is the difference between solids and liquids and a subsidiary theme is a description of the qualities of a solid if dropped.

Passage 12

56. True

   Explanation: the views of the author of the passage are not described so it is true that you cannot tell from it if the author agrees with the vast majority of citizens

57. False

   Explanation: the same criticism is levelled at opposition parties and pressure groups.

58. False

   Explanation: the term 'all time' means never surpassed so an all time low means the lowest on record. You would not normally refer to something as an all time low if it had previously occurred.

59. False

   Explanation: the passage describes bad news as more newsworthy than good news; this does not mean that good news has no news value, only that it is less newsworthy than bad news.

60. Cannot tell

    Explanation: the passage states that public trust in official data is at an all time low but it does not say the public trust in governments, opposition parties, pressure groups and the media is at an all time low and this information cannot be inferred from the passage.

Passage 13

61. False

    Explanation: in the first sentence of the passage it is stated that NASA plans to return to the moon in 15 years but we do not know when the passage was written so we cannot tell how long before the next moon mission. For example the passage may have been written two years ago and therefore the next moon mission will be in 13 years time.

62. True

    Explanation: the passage states 'Another benefit of the polar regions is that they are believed to hold mineral deposits from which oxygen and hydrogen can be extracted. And with oxygen and hydrogen the astronauts will be able to make water.'

63. True

    Explanation: all the listed points are referred to in the passage.

64. Cannot tell

    Explanation: the passage does not provide any details on the sex of the astronauts so by referring to the passage we cannot say if the statement is true or false.

65. False

    Explanation: fatalistic means defeatist and the tone adopted in the passage is not defeatist but upbeat.

Passage 14

66. True
   Explanation: dry is a synonym of arid.

67. True
   Explanation: the passage states that when Australia's interior is mentioned people only think of the arid outback and deserts. The passage then goes on to describe many other habitats including mountains and wetlands.

68. Cannot tell
   Explanation: the passage does not say if the river can still be navigated in a boat nor can we infer this information from it.

69. Cannot tell
   Explanation: the passage does not provide information as to what the author finds most interesting so we cannot tell if the statement is true or false from the information provided in the passage nor can we infer if the statement is true or false.

70. False
   Explanation: sceptical means doubtful or disbelieving and the passage does not adopt a sceptical tone.

Passage 15

71. Cannot tell
   Explanation: the passage provides no information on the effect of any increase in the amount of traffic so we are unable to say if the statement is true or false nor infer from the passage if it is true or false.

72. Cannot tell
   Explanation: the passage does not detail the basis on which the claims in the passage rest and we cannot infer this information from the passage either.

73. False

    Explanation: the passage states that the signs and lights may be removed and does not say that they are to be removed so we cannot infer from the passage that the proposals will go ahead.

74. False

    Explanation: the word principally means mainly.

75. False

    Explanation: cynical means distrusting or sceptical and the passage remains objective, simply describing the new proposal rather than doubting it.

Passage 16

76. False

    Explanation: the passage provides no information about where the raw cotton was grown, only that Manchester was a global centre for the manufacture of cotton cloth.

77. Cannot tell

    Explanation: the date when the passage was written is not provided and if we stick to the information contained in the passage then it is just as plausible that the passage was written at the end of the 20th century.

78. False

    Explanation: the subject of the passage is the city of Manchester, and its architecture is only one of the features of the city that are reviewed.

79. False

    Explanation: you cannot infer that there are other cities in the world called Manchester simply from the fact that the author wrote Manchester, England. The author may have chosen to refer to England for a number of possible reasons. For example, he may have written it in order to help locate the city for any reader who had not heard of it.

80. True

    Explanation: buoyant means cheerful and upbeat and the passage does adopt a buoyant tone regarding the city of Manchester.

Passage 17

81. True

    Explanation: business is a synonym of conglomerate.

82. False

    Explanation: the author argues against the payment of royalties and asserts that the recordings of such works should be free to share.

83. Cannot tell

    Explanation: the views of the author on the issue of physical books rather than digital written works are not provided in the passage. His comments are limited to intellectual property and it may be that he does not extend his argument to property such as physical recordings, books and videos, but we cannot tell from the passage.

84. False

    Explanation: the sentiment of the passage is not about how cultural and creative the public sphere is but that our cultural expression should be free and freely shared.

85. True

    Explanation: the author does present the question of why media conglomerates should be allowed to prosecute people who share music and videos as the basis for the validity of the concluding sentence.

Passage 18

86. False

    Explanation: the passage states that diamonds and graphite are both forms of the element carbon and not that the element carbon has two naturally occurring pure forms. This difference is significant because the statement in the question suggests that carbon has only two forms while the passage simply names two forms (allowing that there are more).

87. False

    Explanation: the passage attributes diamonds with the four qualities: hardness, transparency, occurring naturally and being crystalline in form.

88. False

    Explanation: the passage states there are a great number of carbon-based compounds including many found in living tissue. We cannot infer from this that all living tissue is made up of carbon-based compounds.

89. True

    Explanation: the subject of the passage is the element carbon and its forms.

90. Cannot tell

    Explanation: the passage does not explain why we use carbon fibre to manufacture things that need to be strong but light and it does not state that carbon fibre is stronger than other material of the same weight.

Passage 19

91. True

    Explanation: depression is a disorder of our mental health and the passage states that its frequency increases when there is a mismatch between the demands of modern life and the hours of light and darkness.

92. False

    Explanation: as well as identifying people who live in northern communities, he also identifies people who work shifts or fly distances as at risk. People belonging to these classes could live anywhere.

93. False

    Explanation: the word latitude is used in the phrase 'high latitudes' and this means the northernmost part of the globe.

94. False

    Explanation: the passage does not compare the problems suffered by one group of people (those who work shifts and fly) with another group (people living in northern communities). It compares the problems suffered by two groups: shift workers and long distance flyers with people living in northern communities.

95. Cannot tell

    Explanation: the passage only describes workers as having to get up in winter before it is light. No information is provided regarding school children and we are unable to infer whether or not children too have to get up before it is light (it is possible, for example, that there is no school in winter).

Passage 20

96. True

    Explanation: meaningful is a synonym of significant and spectrum a synonym of range.

97. False

    Explanation: the passage does not contain this statement and so it is false that it is said in the passage. The sentiment of the statement is expressed in the passage but this is not what the question asks.

98. Cannot tell

     Explanation: the passage makes no reference to the content of the school curriculum. It states that children are not taught grammar and punctuation at school because their teachers never learnt it. We cannot infer from this that the curriculum does not contain grammar and punctuation as it is possible that the subject is on the curriculum but simply not taught.

99. True

     Explanation: it is stated in the passage 'in recent years there have been significant improvements in the level of functional literacy amongst school leavers' and so from this we can conclude that the author would agree with the statement made in the question.

100. True

     Explanation: in the passage it is stated that employers complain of far more fundamental failures than placing an adverb in the wrong place or leaving out the prepositional phrase.

Chapter 6: Four full-length realistic practice tests

Practice test 1: Verbal reasoning

1. A
   Explanation: a boat can be powered by sails and a car by its engine.

2. B
   Explanation: one of the products of fire is smoke and words can be used to produce sentences.

3. D
   Explanation: a river runs to the sea and a telephone connects to an exchange.

4. B
   Explanation: smooth is the opposite to fuzzy and interior is the opposite to surface.

5. B
   Explanation: you can be jailed for the crime of fraud and expelled from school for smoking.

6. A
   Explanation: a swan is a type of bird and a mechanical engineer is one of the specialists in that profession.

7. C
   Explanation: polish can be described as waxy and baby food as mushy.

8. C
   Explanation: height and weight are two forms of measurement and joyous and sombre are two forms of sentiment.

9. D
   Explanation: to guess is to estimate something and to inflate something is to expand it.

10. B

Explanation: stupid is the opposite of sensible and transparent is the opposite of opaque.

11. A

Explanation: a book is made of pages and a cloth is made of yarns (both pages and yarns are made of fibres).

12. D

Explanation: in order to be played a violin needs a bow and to operate a lock a key is needed.

13. C

Explanation: barley is a type of cereal and Parliament is a type of assembly.

14. C

Explanation: photosynthesis requires sunlight and a concert requires an orchestra.

15. C

Explanation: acid and alkali are opposites and strict is the opposite of lax.

16. B

Explanation: languages are used to communicate and a microscope to magnify.

17. D

Explanation: both pairs of words have similar meanings.

18. C

Explanation: proponent and supporter mean the same, as do myth and story.

19. A

Explanation: hockey is a ballgame and a painkiller is a type of medicine.

20. D

Explanation: both pairs of words are opposites.

21. B

    Explanation: geology is a branch of science and statistics a branch of mathematics.

22. C

    Explanation: a set square and a ruler are instruments used in geometry and an oblong and cuboid are types of geometric shape.

23. A

    Explanation: refuse is another way of saying decline and dilute is an alternative way to describe weakening something.

24. D

    Explanation: construction and transport are both types of industry and turtles and lizards are two types of reptile.

25. A

    Explanation: flyover and viaduct are types of bridge and Archbishop and Ayatollah are two types of religious leader.

26. 2

    Explanation: tabloid and broadsheet are types of newspaper and Spanish and Hindi are types of language.

27. 4

    Explanation: both pairs comprise an item and a product of it. Candles produce light and waves produce surf.

28. 1

    Explanation: both describe an item and one of its principal components. Furniture can contain wood and a pencil lead is often graphite.

29. 4

    Explanation: the relationship is an item and its effect. Medicine can produce a cure and a fire warmth (insulation cannot produce warmth only help retain it).

30. 4

   Explanation: the relationship is one of an item and what it is made of. A house can be made of bricks and a pension a series of monthly or weekly contributions.

31. 3

   Explanation: the relationship is that of what potential an item has. A seed can grow into a plant and an inference can lead to a conclusion.

32. 4

   Explanation: both pairs are opposites.

33. 1

   Explanation: the relationship is one of an item that makes another possible. Many animals need air to breathe and a solution is only possible if you first have a problem.

34. 2

   Explanation: both pairs comprise words with similar meanings.

35. 1

   Explanation: the relationship is one of an important tool and the activity in which it is used. A pencil is used extensively in art and a telephone in telecommunications.

36. 3

   Explanation: the relationship is the negative effect of something. The sun can burn you and criticism can make you angry.

37. 1

   Explanation: the relationship is words that sound the same but have different meanings and spellings.

38. 2

   Explanation: the relationship is one of potential. Music has the potential to please and research to make discoveries.

39. 1

   Explanation: the pairs are opposites.

40. 4

Explanation: both pairs are opposites

Practice test 2: Verbal reasoning

1. 4

Explanation: headlong and hurried are the closest in meaning from the list of options (none is the opposite of hurried).

2. 2

Explanation: to prevent something is to avoid it happening; prevention and avoidance are synonyms.

3. 3

Explanation: decisive and deceptive are neither synonyms nor antonyms, but deceptive and truthful are antonyms so the answer is 3.

4. 3

Explanation: investigate and ignore are opposites.

5. 1

Explanation: closest in meaning.

6. 2

Explanation: unorthodox and probable are neither synonyms nor antonyms, but probable and credible are synonyms so the answer is 2.

7. 1

Explanation: if you assess something then you evaluate it.

8. 4

Explanation: relationship and habitually are neither synonyms nor antonyms, but habitually and seldom are opposites so the answer is 4.

9. 3

Explanation: remain means the opposite of escape.

10. 1

Explanation: closest in meaning.

11. 4

    Explanation: regulations is a synonym of code.

12. 3

    Explanation: closest in meaning.

13. 4

    Explanation: negative means the opposite of affirmative.

14. 3

    Explanation: idea and thorough are neither synonyms nor antonyms, but thorough and methodical are synonyms so the answer is 3.

15. 2

    Explanation: to support something is to brace it.

16. 2

    Explanation: open and unused are neither synonyms nor antonyms, but unused and pristine are synonyms.

17. 3

    Explanation: consult means the opposite of ignore (if you ignore someone you may insult them, but ignore does not mean the same as insult).

18. 1

    Explanation: closest in meaning.

19. 2

    Explanation: comfort and solemn are neither synonyms nor antonyms, but solemn and informal are antonyms.

20. 4

    Explanation: deploy and utilize are synonyms.

21. 4

    Explanation: fiscal and economical are neither synonym nor antonym but economical and careful are synonyms.

22. 1

    Explanation: neighbourly and sociable are synonyms.

23. 1

Explanation: opposites.

24. 2

Explanation: deluge means the opposite of drought.

25. 4

Explanation: tangible and untangle are neither synonyms nor antonyms but untangle and entangle are opposites.

26. 3

Explanation: liberate means the opposite of enslave.

27. 2

Explanation: harm and restrain are neither antonyms nor synonyms, but harm and injure are synonyms.

28. 2

Explanation: conceal means the opposite of forthright.

29. 3

Explanation: closest in meaning.

30. 4

Explanation: ordeal and affliction are synonyms.

31. 3

Explanation: speedy and composure are neither synonyms nor antonyms, but panic and composure are opposites.

32. 2

Explanation: collapse and disintegrate are synonyms.

33. 1

Explanation: interrupt and continue are opposites.

34. 1

Explanation: extinguish and quench are synonyms.

35. 4

   Explanation: exile and refuge are neither synonyms nor antonyms, but refuge and protection are synonyms.

Test 3: Verbal usage

1. D, been waiting and it left
    Explanation: the sentence makes sense with either the past simple 'waited' or past continuous 'been waiting', but only the past simple, left, is correct (remember it's is the abbreviation of it is).

2. A, haven't and tomorrow
    Explanation: suggested answer A is the only option that offers a credible match between events and intentions.

3. D, [no word needed] and the
    Explanation: when we want to specify which person, job title or place we are referring to we use the article 'the'. We use the article 'a' to indicate that we do not know the person or thing; we do not use an article if we know the person or thing.

4. C, ice-cold and ice-cream
    Explanation: ice-cold and ice-cream are both hyphenated.

5. B, might and shan't
    Explanation: might implies something is less likely to happen than may; we use shan't to describe a negative situation.

6. A, that survived and were destroyed
    Explanation: the correct form is that survived and were destroyed; answers B and C are impossible as well as incorrect in their construction.

7. C, much and have got to
    Explanation: 'really must' and 'am going to' imply in this context that 'I want to', while 'have got to' suggests an obligation. 'Have got to' is preferred when future arrangements are obligatory.

8. B, woman and women
Explanation: the woman (singular female) doctor only treats women (plural).

9. B, to and on
Explanation: 'to' implies movement; 'at,' 'on' and 'in' imply position.

10. D, made
Explanation: because it is stated that the friend is new it is better to choose D 'I made a new friend...'.

11. B, used not to be
Explanation: only B makes sense given the opening clause of the sentence that implies that a cure has recently been found.

12. C, needn't have gone
Explanation: it is clear from the sentence that the person had gone to the trouble of cooking and so we say needn't have gone. You didn't need to go is incorrect because it fails to acknowledge that the person did cook the food, and it doesn't tie in with the past tense 'cooked'.

13. A, at
Explanation: we say we are angry with a person but at an event or something.

14. D, aside from
Explanation: 'aside from,' 'except,' 'but for' and 'but' are all used to introduce an exception – in this case a time when crude was more expensive, but only aside from is correct given the structure of the sentence.

15. B, for
Explanation: the verb to care is usually followed by the preposition about or for but in this instance only care for makes good sense.

16. C, at and on
Explanation: we use at to refer to the time, on to refer to the day or date, and we say in the month of the year.

17. A, There is and it
    Explanation: when we introduce something we use the phrase there is or the abbreviation there's; in subsequent reference we use it. Theirs means possessions of someone.

18. D, harder and more intelligent
    Explanation: when drawing comparisons we add 'er' to short words but use more (or less) in front of long words.

19. D, any and some
    Explanation: we use any in a negative situation and some to make a positive point.

20. B, who and that
    Explanation: who and whom are used to refer to people while which and that refer to objects.

21. C, so and big and red
    Explanation: we say so and such for emphasis, but we use so with adjectives. We usually put adjectives in the order of size then colour rather than the other way around.

22. B, them
    Explanation: them is plural and identifies that two sisters are older than the boy.

23. D, at and by
    Explanation: we say at a beach and that we travelled by bus; we also say on the beach but not on bus.

24. A, so and as
    Explanation: as is used to make a comparison while so is used for emphasis.

25. B, apologize and best
    Explanation: we correctly say to apologize and she apologized but not to apologized or apology/ies. Best is correct in this instance but better would also be correct if the sentence read it would be better if she did.

26. C, academic's and on

Explanation: the possessive singular form academic's is correct in this situation and serves to identify whose speech it is that has been left on the plane. We say on a plane but in a car and at a party.

27. C, much and many

Explanation: we use much in the case of singular uncountable nouns and many in the case of plural countable nouns.

28. B, late and slow

Explanation: we say a train is early or late but that a watch is fast or slow. We can identify B as correct because the only sensible answer requires the train to be early and the watch to be slow. Notice that the sentence starts with although, which means in spite of the fact.

29. C, I had been wanting and on paying

Explanation: the sentence can correctly start with either suggested answers C and D but only suggested answer C offers the correct structure for the second part of the sentence.

30. A, less and first

Explanation: both first and last are correct but we use less when the noun is uncountable.

31. B, I'd and wouldn't

Explanation: I'd is the abbreviation for I had or I would; wouldn't is the abbreviation for would not.

32. D, unconditional and non-starter

Explanation: words beginning in 'un' are not usually hyphenated while those beginning with 'non' usually are.

33. B, latest and loose

Explanation: the assignment is not her last as another awaits her so we say latest; lose means lost while loose in this context means set free.

34. D, principle and take a number and I will call back

    Explanation: principle is correct in this context and means adherence to a moral code (principal means main idea or chief person); we can correctly refer back to someone with their, them, or they.

35. C, where and whereby

    Explanation: where refers to a location or other relationship and whereby means by which (where could be used in both positions but this option is not offered).

Test 4: Reading comprehension and critical reasoning

Passage 1

1. True

   Explanation: this is a reasonable summary of the passage. The new markets are those of the service industries and they were once considered safe because it used to be thought that the service provider needed to be near the customer.

2. True

   Explanation: it is stated in the passage that, 'service providers in Europe and the United States have struggled to compete because of the regulatory burden and high wages'.

3. False

   Explanation: the passage makes no reference to whether or not India's economic growth is sustainable and so it is false to say that the passage suggests that it is unsustainable.

4. Cannot tell

   Explanation: the passage does not provide a view on the relative value of jobs in the various sectors so we are unable to tell if this statement is true or false.

5. False

    Explanation: from the passage we can infer that the author would agree that there is little we can do to stop the loss of jobs.

Passage 2

6. False

    Explanation: an inconvenience is a nuisance or irritation. In the passage the lack of transport is described in stronger terms than this.

7. True

    Explanation: the term essential workers does not occur in the passage.

8. True

    Explanation: the passage states that no other European country closes its public transport over the period and from this we can infer that Britain is unique in Europe in this respect.

9. Cannot tell

    Explanation: the passage does not provide information on whether or not the authorities would run a service if the government paid them to and this information cannot be inferred from the passage.

10. False

    Explanation: the passage states that the authorities do not run a service over Christmas because they believe it would not make a profit. From this we can infer that they run public transport not in order to provide a service but to make a profit.

Passage 3

11. Cannot tell

    Explanation: in fact Facebook is an example of a social networking site but we cannot establish this from the passage so the correct answer to the question is cannot tell.

12. True

    Explanation: the three groups are users, software developers and advertisers.

13. True

    Explanation: it is stated in the passage that 'the site owner obviously wants to make money, so targets advertisers willing to pay in order to market to the millions of users'.

14. True

    Explanation: a synonym of energetic is vigorous.

15. True

    Explanation: the tone of a passage is its attitude or character, and overall the passage presents the challenges as teething troubles that when resolved will ensure successful advertising-funded social network sites.

Passage 4

16. False

    Explanation: inflation is an antonym of deflation; surplus means excess or spare.

17. True

    Explanation: the two advantages described are a reduction in trade surpluses and the offset of some of the increase in the cost of imported commodities.

18. False

    Explanation: the first sentence of the passage states that 'current levels of domestic inflation make it a lot easier for the government of China to accept a stronger domestic currency'. If that level were to be 5 per cent then the fact that the current levels make it easier to accept a stronger currency would not change.

19. False

    Explanation: in the first sentence of the passage we are informed that the domestic currency of China is the Yuan.

20. False

    Explanation: it is clear from the passage that it is now a lot easier for the government of China to accept a stronger domestic currency but it is not clear from the passage that they have allowed the currency to appreciate.

Passage 5

21. False

    Explanation: the author does not state that he does not accept that the burning of fossil fuels is causing an increase in concentrations of carbon dioxide.

22. True

    Explanation: the passage does not detail an occasion when the scientists' forecasts were proved to be false but argues that in practice the scientists rarely look to see if their forecasts are true or false.

23. False

    Explanation: standpoint means point of view and the passage is written from the point of view that unverifiable predictions may cause alarm, be newsworthy and change people's behaviour but they may not be based on good scientific methods.

24. Cannot tell

    Explanation: sceptical means to doubt. The passage does not provide details of the author's experience and whether or not it makes him doubt how environmental forecasting is being used.

25. False

    Explanation: unproven is the antonym of verified; a synonym would be confirmed.

Passage 6

26. False

    Explanation: the main point of the passage is that we should buy more locally produced fresh food and prepare our meals ourselves.

27. Cannot tell

    Explanation: the passage does not state whether the most convenient food is also the cheapest (note reference to the cheapest only occurs in question 26 and not in the passage). Nor is the most convenient food described as expensive so we cannot tell from the information provided in the passage if this statement is true or false.

28. False

    Explanation: the passage states that people often lack the skills and knowledge to turn back to good food. We can infer that this means turn back from the industrially produced meals to locally sourced food that we prepare ourselves.

29. Cannot tell

    Explanation: the passage does not provide information on the specific consequences for public health or the components in industrially produced foods that cause them.

30. True

    Explanation: the author states, 'we treat food like fuel. We seek out the most convenient' and that 'we eat it in a hurry and on the move rather than together around a table'. These sentiments are consistent with the view that we do not respect food enough.

Passage 7

31. False

    Explanation: the number of children who took part in the survey is not detailed in the passage and cannot be inferred from it.

32. True

    Explanation: it is stated in the passage that 'on average the children spent $23 a week and over a third of this was spent on sugary and fatty foods and drinks.' From this we can tell that the sizeable amount spent on these items amounted to less than half the total pocket money.

33. Cannot tell

    Explanation: no information is provided that allows us to determine which age group of children are the biggest spenders so we cannot tell if the statement is true or false.

34. True

    Explanation: a survey is a type of investigation and is also called a study.

35. False

    Explanation: the author is describing the finding of a survey and not attempts to solve a problem.

Passage 8

36. False

    Explanation: the passage is about the failure of our international institutions and treaties to provide global authority.

37. True

    Explanation: the passage does not mention potential solutions only the failure of global governance, so it cannot be said to touch on them.

38. Cannot tell

    Explanation: the passage does not detail what is required to address the identified failure of global governance. It may be possible that the existing international organizations and treaties could be effective if amended, and this possibility means that we cannot infer from the passage that an entirely new system of global governance is required.

39. True

    Explanation: it is stated in the passage that all too often efforts to address the many common challenges are pulled down by narrow national interests, and from this we can infer that failure to tackle common threats is attributed to national interests.

40. False

    Explanation: the term interdependence is used in the passage but its meaning is not explained or defined.

An interpretation of your score in the practice tests

A score over 25 in any one of the tests

Your score suggests a high level of ability and confidence in verbal reasoning. You have demonstrated sustained concentration and an ability to work quickly and under pressure.

Concentrate the remaining time you have for further practice on material relevant to other aspects of the recruitment process that you face so that you can be sure you can perform to this high standard in all aspects of the challenge.

A score of 20 or above in any one of the tests

This is a good score if you secured it in test 4 and a score on which you can improve in tests 1–3. In the real test the bulk of candidates are likely to score somewhere in this category. Your score may be sufficient to get you through to the next stage of most recruitment processes. But it will depend on the number of other candidates and vacancies and your precise position in relation to the performance of others.

If you found you did not have sufficient time to complete all the questions then speed up. You might try risking getting a few more wrong because you do not double-check your answers, but that way you will have more time to attempt more questions. Alternatively, practise at better managing your time during the test and avoid spending too long on questions that you find difficult.

If you found it hard to maintain the level of concentration demanded by the practice test, this is entirely normal. At the end of tests like these you should feel completely wiped out. If you don't then you are not making the required effort. Remember that even a very able candidate, if they are to do well in tests like these, has to try very hard. Make yourself keep going right until you hear 'Put your pencil down' or the clock runs out of time on the computer screen.

Undertake more practice and see if you can improve that bit more. If you can then you might succeed in pulling yourself further ahead of the majority of candidates and be more sure of a positive result.

A score below 15 in any one of the tests

Before you take the next test, go over the questions you got wrong and the explanations, and try to work out where you went wrong. It helps to get someone else's opinion. Such a review will greatly assist you to understand the demands of these types of test.

Once you have completed a thorough review, take a break, overnight preferably, and get yourself into a really determined mindset. Find a quiet space and enough time and take the next test, only this time really go for it and practise what you learnt from the last test; prove to yourself that you can do better. You might well be pleasantly surprised with the next result. If you manage a better score on your next attempt then you have made an important discovery. You have realized that you have what it takes to do well in these tests and you now appreciate what you have to do to do well in these tests.

Now set aside a quite significant amount of time for further practice. Seek out other titles in the Kogan Page Testing Series containing this sort of question, and make it a habit to read a quality newspaper every day, and economic and political weekly journals.

Take encouragement from the fact that with practice you can show dramatic improvements in your score in this type of sub-test. In time you will gain further in confidence, accuracy and speed. It will take time but if the opportunity towards which you are working is something you really want, then simply go for it. You have already begun the process of dramatically improving your score, so take encouragement. The vast majority of candidates will discover the hard way that they need more practice by failing a real test. You are already ahead of them so track down sufficient practice material on which to work, get started in plenty of time and you will go on to pass something you might otherwise have failed.

ALSO AVAILABLE FROM KOGAN PAG

ISBN: 978 0 7494 4969 8
Paperback 2008

ISBN: 978 0 7494 5229 2
Paperback 2008

ISBN: 978 0 7494 4421 1
Paperback 2005

ISBN: 978 0 7494 5064 9
Paperback 2007

Buy online at:
www.koganpage.com